SAS TACTICAL VEHICLE OPERATIONS

TACTICAL DRIVING, INTERDICTION, AND COMMANDEERING

Australian SASR Counter Terror Operations Manual

Copyright © 2017 Varangian Press

All rights reserved.

ISBN: 1981901094
ISBN-13 9781981901098

DISCLAIMER

This book is intended for information purposes only. The information contained in this book is true and complete to the best of our knowledge. The author and publisher disclaim any liability in connection with the use of this information.

INFATUO MODO DISCIT AB EXPERIENTIA

"A fool learns only from experience"

Roman Proverb

CONTENTS

BRIEF HISTORY OF THE SAS

The SASR can trace its beginnings back to the Australian Z Special Unit and Independent Commando Companies that fought during the Second World War. On 25 July 1957, the 1st Special Air Service Company, Royal Australian Infantry, was raised at Campbell Barracks, Swanbourne, in Western Australia; largely modelled on the British SAS.

"The Company consisted of a headquarters and four platoons comprising about 200 all ranks by the time it became part of The Royal Australian Regiment in 1960." At the same time it was given responsibility for commando and SF operations in the Australian Army.

On 04 September 1964, the 1st Special Air Service Company was expanded to become the Special Air Service Regiment with three sabre squadrons. Following disengagement from Vietnam in October 1971, 2 Squadron was disbanded to allow the SAS Training Squadron to be raised (later renamed the SAS Support Squadron, subsequently the Operational Support Squadron).

The SASR gained its CT remit on 23 February 1978 after a terrorist attack on the Sydney Hilton on the 13 February in the same year. In order to maintain the SASRs CT and war role capabilities, in 1982 the disbanded 2 Squadron was reformed.

CHAPTER 1

VEHICLE COUNTER AND ANTI SURVEILLANCE

INTRODUCTION

This manual is designed for personnel who may come under hostile surveillance or attack while operating a motor vehicle. Whether the attack is an attempted arrest, carjacking, kidnapping, or terrorist assassination, the response is the same, to get out of the situation quickly. The goal is to help train the driver how to use his vehicle as a means of escape or weapon for survival.

By carefully studying this manual, the driver will learn what a car is capable of and most importantly, his own limits. He will be shown how hard it is to stop a moving vehicle, and he will be taught evasive manoeuvres such as forward and reverse spins and ramming. The driver will be taught how to drive at high speed and at night with or without Night Observation Devices.

These skills are vital for the success of the mission and for the survival of the operator upon catastrophic compromise.

As simply reading the manual is no substitute for practical, hands-on experience, personnel should not undertake the techniques and procedures described herein unless supervised by a qualified Tactical Vehicle Instructor.

VEHICLE COUNTER AND ANTI-SURVEILLANCE

Prior to any assassination, arrest or capture attempt, an adversary is sure to practice at least rudimentary vehicle surveillance to either determine your movements for intelligence purposes or to direct their comrades to your position so you can be killed or captured.

Even considering the volume of vehicles on modern roads, especially in urban areas, vehicle surveillance is reasonably simple to detect and even easier to annul. Please keep in mind that an adversary who is intent on capturing or killing you on the spot will not be content to stay clandestine. They will go overt at the drop of a hat and actively pursue you. See other parts of this manual for techniques to negate overt pursuit.

Vehicle Surveillance Threat Overview

Vehicle surveillance may be undertaken using only one vehicle or using two or more vehicles. One-vehicle surveillance suffers from one major drawback - The target has to be kept in view at all times and followed by the same vehicle. Surveillance operators can try to overcome this disadvantage somewhat by changing seating arrangements within the vehicle; putting on and taking off hats, coats, and sunglasses; changing license plates; and turning off onto side streets and then turning back to resume the tail. This makes it necessary for a person suspecting surveillance to remember aspects of a following vehicle that cannot easily be changed such as the make, model, and color of the car and any body damage such as rust, dents, etc.

The use of two or more vehicles permits surveillance teams to switch positions or to drop out of the surveillance when necessary. One vehicle follows the target vehicle and directs other vehicles by radio.

The other vehicle may follow behind the lead surveillance vehicle, precede the target vehicle, or travel on parallel roads. At intersections, the vehicle following directly behind the target vehicle will generally travel straight ahead while alerting all other vehicles of the direction in which the target vehicle has turned. Another vehicle in the formation will then take a position behind the target and become the lead vehicle, taking over the responsibility for giving instructions to other surveillance

operators. The former lead vehicle then makes a U-turn or travels around the block to take up a new position ready to resume the lead vehicle position again when necessary.

People who have well-established routines permit surveillance teams to use methods that are much more difficult to detect. If, for example, you leave your usual place of work at the same time each day and travel by the most direct route to your home or if you live in a remote area with a few or no alternate routes to your home, the surveillance team has no need to follow you all the way to your residence. An alternative method of surveillance in such situations is leading surveillance and progressive surveillance.

In leading surveillance a surveillance operator travels in front of the target while the observer watches for turns. When the target turns, this is noted. The next day the surveillance operator makes a turn where the target did the previous day. Over a period of time the surveillance team will discover the entire route to the residence while still driving in a position that creates much less suspicion.

There are two forms of progressive surveillance. In the first form, surveillance vehicles are placed at intersections along the probable routes of the target. When the target makes a turn, this is noted and the position of the surveillance team is adjusted to check the next intersection. Eventually, this method leads the surveillance team to the residence.

In the second form of progressive surveillance, a vehicle will follow the target for a short distance and then turn off. On successive days a surveillance operator picks up the target where he or she left off the previous day. Leading and progressive surveillance are extremely difficult to detect, but you should not give anyone the opportunity to use these methods.

If the surveillance team loses sight of or contact with the target, they will conduct what is known as a grid search. This involves systematically searching each possible exit route the target may have taken, starting from the point where contact was initially lost. It is advantageous for the target to allow as much time as possible to elapse between the final contact point and the start of a grid search. A grid search is initially highly effective, but as time passes its chances of success reduce dramatically as the target is given more opportunity to slip the net.

Detecting Vehicle Surveillance

Vehicle surveillance is a very difficult operation for an adversary to carry out successfully without detection.

The most effective methods for detecting most forms of vehicle surveillance are:

1. Being alert for strangers or unusual cars at the start of a journey.

2. Note vehicles which are not familiar in your street or area. A good Mnemonic to remember when noting vehicle details is: "CYMBALS"
   C Colour

   YYear

   MMake

   B Body
   AAdditional Accessories

   LLicence Plate

   SState of Registration

3. Note and closely observe any vehicle which consistently drives too close or maintains an excessive distance behind your vehicle.

4. Note any vehicles that behave in an erratic manner (change lanes frequently, run red lights and stop signs, etc.)

5. Observe and make a mental note of any vehicles that change direction with you.

6. Drive slower than the flow of traffic and observe for vehicles doing the same.

7. Concentrate on observing vehicles parking and departing at the same times as you.

8. Vehicles which do not indicate when changing lanes or turning corners.

9. Stop in a sparsely settled area to see if anyone else stops.

10. Drive up a dead-end street to see if anyone is following. If not, stop and exit the vehicle momentarily, then re-enter and drive out of the street again.

11. Do a quick U-turn, then repeat the procedure, looking for the same vehicles parked in an over watch position of the entrance to the street.

In each case, watch for the reactions of any vehicles that you may suspect. Any vehicles that make unusual maneuvers should be carefully noted. Do not forget to check for motorcycles or motorbikes, since in many parts of the world they seem to be favoured by surveillance operators because they move easily through heavy traffic.

Detecting surveillance requires a constant state of alertness and must become an unconscious habit. We do not want to encourage paranoia, but a good sense of what is normal and what is unusual in your surroundings could be more important than any other type of security precaution you take. Above all, do not hesitate to report or act on any unusual events.

Counter-Vehicle Surveillance Techniques

Counter surveillance is the application of techniques to identify and counteract possible surveillance. This is done in three stages:

Detect

Identify

Revise activity or continue

Do not let your actions confirm counter surveillance.

Countersurveillance methods will negate the element of surprise for an adversary. The purpose of counter-surveillance is not to "ditch" surveillance, rather it is used to covertly gather intelligence on or "direct" a surveillance team through deception and various ruses, which can turn the situation to your advantage.

Keeping firmly in mind the three stages illustrated above, basic counter-surveillance methods include:

1. Using "corridors" and "choke points".

2. Stopping to check road map and noting vehicles that pass.

3. Stopping due to "engine problems" and noting vehicles that pass.
4. Use a support person to observe for indicators or suspicious activity.

5. Avoiding regular arrival and departure times.

6. Varying the route you take when traveling to common destinations.

Anti-Vehicle Surveillance Techniques

Anti-surveillance is the application of techniques designed to evade a surveillance team.

Basic anti-surveillance techniques include:

1.	Running traffic lights.

2.	U turns.

3.	Alternatively driving slowly then quickly.

4.	Driving slowly for a long period of time.

5.	Driving against traffic in one way streets

6.	Driving into dead-end streets and cul de sacs.

7.	Driving quickly, and then stopping in a blind location to observe other vehicles come past at speed.

8.	Driving around the block from the suspected surveillance start point.

9.	Driving into and straight out of a parking area.

10.	Turning without indicating or turning a corner from the wrong lane.

For the above methods to be most effective it is imperative to keep an adversary in the dark about the fact that surveillance has been detected. If the adversary has been given no indication that their surveillance has been compromised, it is far easier for the target to just disappear.

CHAPTER 2

VEHICLE DYNAMICS AND PHYSICS

Basic Vehicle Dynamics Theory

One of the most important concepts to master with high-performance driving is the concept of the vehicle as a platform. If a driver can begin to picture the overall vehicle as a stable object, the process of high-performance driving becomes easier. This is sometimes a difficult process to develop, but once an operator masters the concept, high-performance driving problems decrease and overall vehicle control increases dramatically.

Weight Transfer

The main component of understanding vehicle dynamics is to study the effects of weight transfer on a vehicle. Every time a vehicle accelerates, decelerates or changes direction, the weight distribution of the vehicle is altered. This distribution of weight across the platform is known as weight transfer.

When practicing high-performance evasive or offensive driving, it is critical that the driving platform is kept level or stable throughout all aspects of vehicle operation. This means that whether the vehicle is accelerating, decelerating or changing direction, the operator needs to be constantly aware of the effects of weight transfer and the potential benefits and risks that such transfers present.

A major concept of understanding weight transfer is to look at the effects of shifting weight on the stability of the vehicle. If the vehicle is simply viewed as an object, this is much easier.

In the following diagram, compare each object:

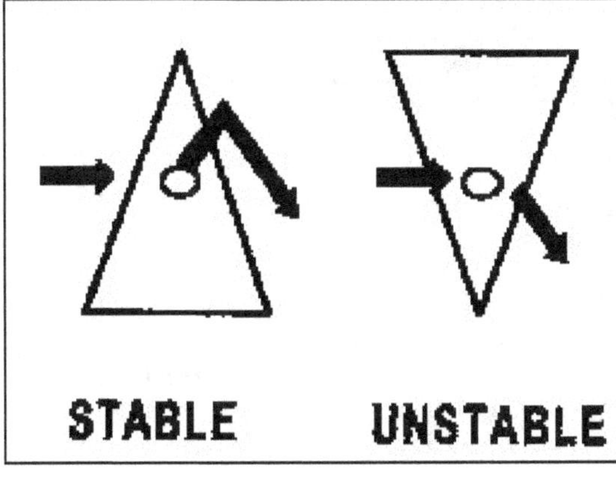

- A stable object must rise at the centre of gravity before it falls

- An unstable object will fall when force is exerted

Axis of motion affects the vehicle's weight distribution:

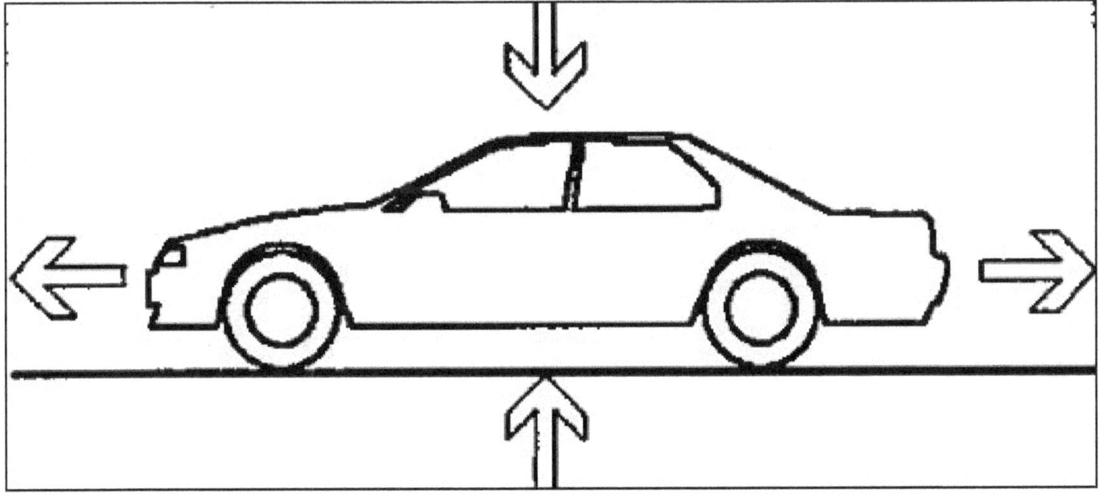

Pitch is motion from front to back on a horizontal plane. Pitch is the axis of motion most affected by straight travel.

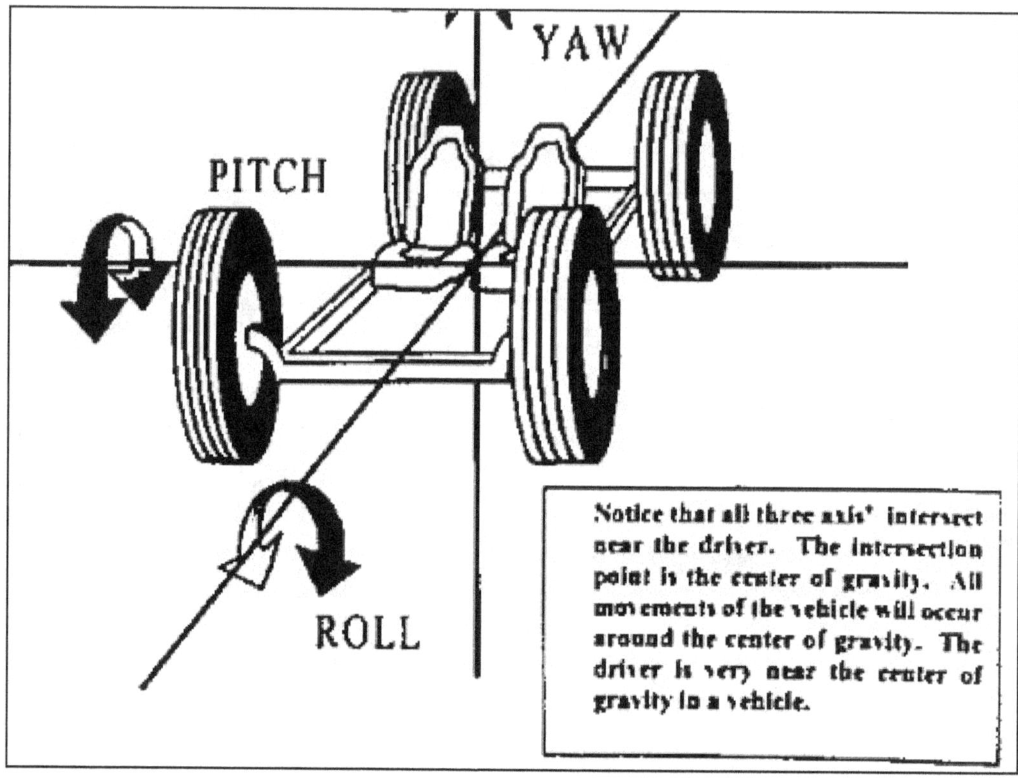

When the vehicle is at rest, the vehicle's weight is evenly distributed and it is most stable. This is also true of a vehicle moving at a constant speed in a straight line.

Letting off the accelerator or applying the brakes moves weight to the front of the vehicle.

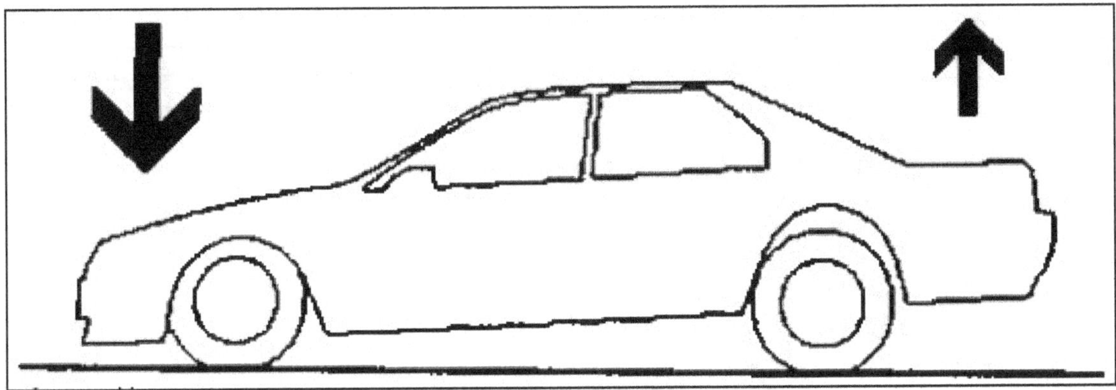

Releasing the brakes or applying the accelerator moves weight to the rear of the vehicle.

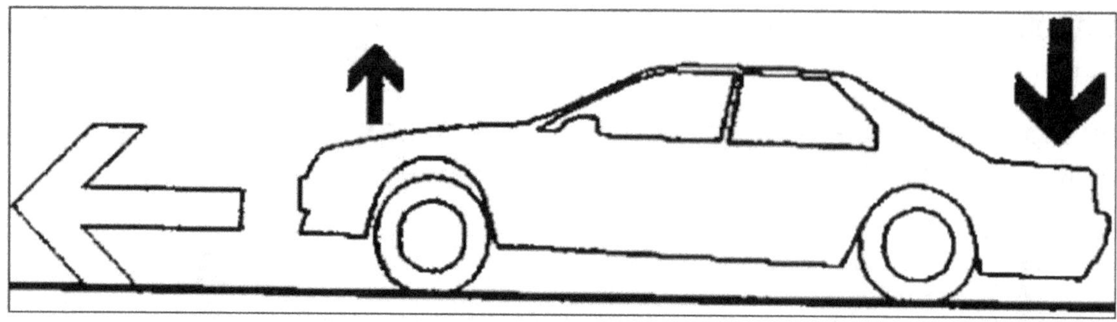

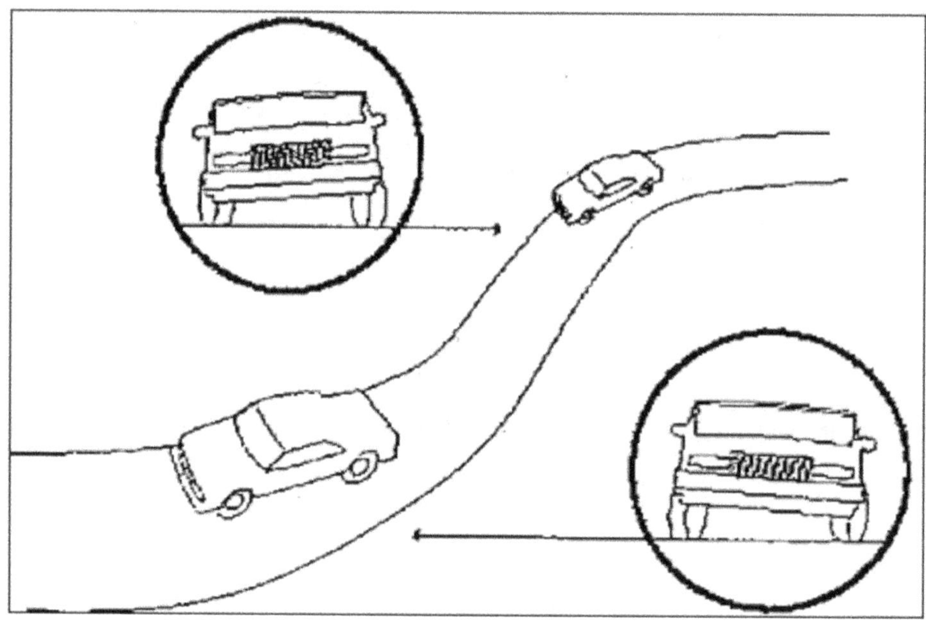

Changing directions shifts weight from side to side.

The final major concept of understanding the vehicle as a flat and stable platform is a basic understanding of what effects the vehicle suspension and design have on vehicle control. To better grasp the effects of suspension, consider the following:

Energy is stored in the suspension during a turn, through a curve, under braking and under acceleration.

Stored energy must be dissipated.

Energy stored in a spring is an example of potential energy.

The key to controlling the release of potential energy is smooth steering.

As the operator masters the concepts of weight transfer and vehicle platform stability, he/she will begin to make weight shifts and transfers smooth, not rough or jerky.

A few notes on vehicle suspension:

The purpose of a suspension system is to:

Balance the forces during a change in direction or velocity.

Smooth out weight transfer

Keep all four wheels firmly on the ground.

Keep the vehicle flat and level.

Platform stability is intimately linked to weight transfer. Platform stability can only be accomplished by smooth steady acceleration and deceleration, slowing down and making smooth steering inputs.

Turning Dynamics

Simply turning the front tyres of a vehicle will induce a braking effect. The diagram below is used to help explain why this occurs and to help the operator begin to understand the effectiveness of the trail braking concept to help balance the vehicle.

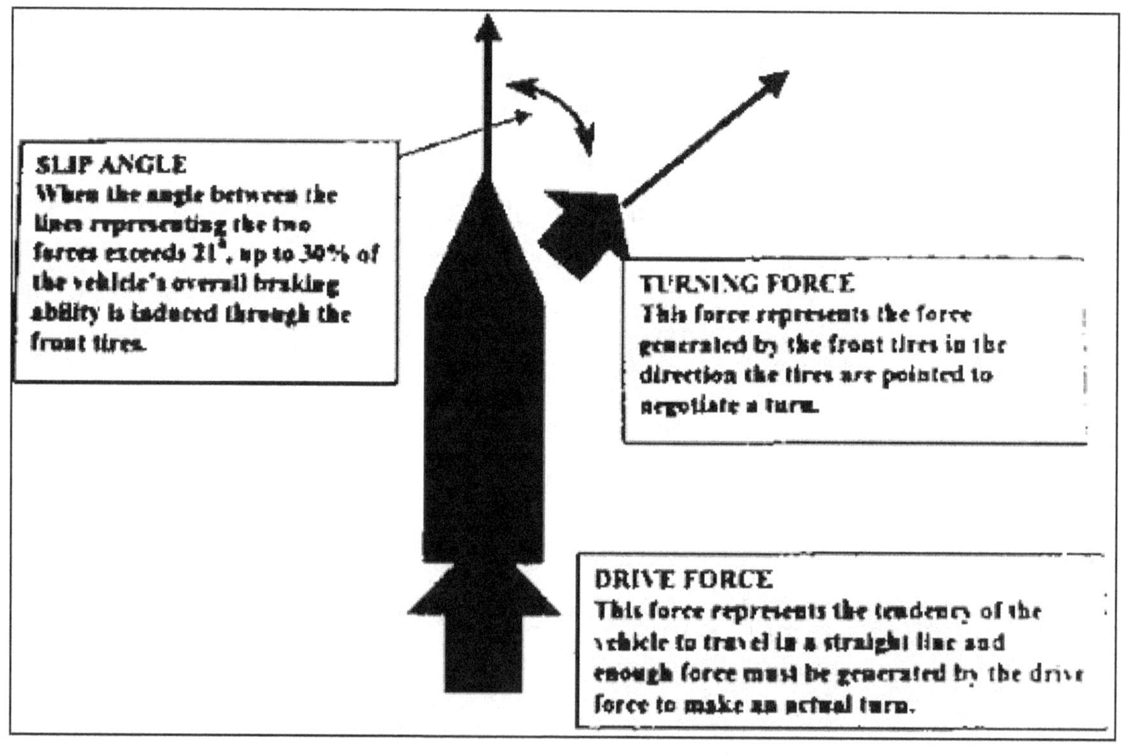

The Physical Laws of Motion

The physical laws of motion are absolute and effect vehicle operation. Understanding of these laws will help the operator to understand why vehicles act as they do in certain circumstances and may help to control the effects of these physical laws.

1. *"EVERY BODY OF MASS CONTINUES IN A STATE OF REST OR UNIFORM MOTION IN A STRAIGHT LINE UNLESS IT IS COMPELLED TO CHANGE THAT STATE BY FORCES*

   IMPRESSED UPON IT."

This is otherwise known as INERTIA. A vehicle once set in motion will continue to move in a straight line unless compelled to do otherwise. In order to change the direction of the vehicle, we develop rotational (rolling) friction with the front tyres, which compels the front tyres to

change direction. If rotational friction is lost, sliding friction is induced and the vehicle will travel in the direction the center of mass was headed.

2. *"THE ACCELERATION OF A BODY OF MASS IS DIRECTLY*

   PROPORTIONAL TO THE NET FORCE ACTING ON THE BODY AND INVERSELY PROPORTIONAL TO THE MASS OF THE

   BODY."

Application of this physical law on vehicles is actually quite simple. A vehicle with a large amount of mass and a small engine will function like a vehicle with a small amount of mass and a large engine. The best combination is when mass is balanced by engine size.

3. "TO EVERY ACTION FORCE, THERE IS AN OPPOSITE REACTION FORCE."

The third law of motion is best described by comparing the forces, which occur when a vehicle attempts to change direction. A center-seeking, or centripetal force is working against a center-fleeing, or centrifugal force. If these forces balance, cornering occurs.

The Most Important Considerations of the Laws of Motion:

The first and third laws of motion are the most important in overall vehicle control. The faster you go, the longer it will take to stop or change direction.

The driver only controls two things in a vehicle –

1. *Speed*
2. *Direction*

The laws of motion will always influence the amount of vehicle control the operator has available.

CHAPTER 3

DRIVING TECHNIQUES

Driving Position

The operator's position in the seat is critical is his/her ability to control the vehicle properly. Many drivers do not naturally sit in the proper position. The objective is for the driver to be situated where he or she has maximum support for cornering, easy to control accelerator, brake and clutch pedals and complete ability to fully turn the steering wheel. .

Upon entering the vehicle, the driver should adjust the seat cushion so that he or she is "in it" as far as possible. Next, the driver should slide the seat so that clutch can be pushed all the way to the floor with some bend still in the operator's knee. Finally, the operator should adjust the seat back so that he or she is able to sit their wrists on the top of the steering wheel. A good test for correct seating position is to grasp the wheel at the "10 to 2" position and turning the wheel 90 to 180 degrees to the left and right without the driver pulling their shoulders away from the seat back. The elbows should still have a little bend in them. The steering wheel should be held with the thumbs resting on the inside rim of the wheel, not tightly wrapped around it. This technique allows the driver to use their arm muscles to control the steering wheel, not the wrists.

Using the above guidelines, it can be a little disconcerting for a student high-performance driver as they will feel they are too close to the wheel. The position is correct and gives a greater degree of control than is available to the basic civilian driver who sits further back and grasps the steering wheel by the top and bottom.

Ocular driving

The average civilian driver has little appreciation of how important their vision is: more specifically, where to look while driving. Most drivers on the street usually don't look far enough ahead. The operator should try to ignore their natural tendencies and always have their eyes one step ahead.

The operator should read the road ahead, using the line of road markers, trees, telephone poles, etc. to give a good indication of the direction of any curves or turns in the road as well as crests and grades. The operator should keep looking ahead as far as he/she can see. The further you can look ahead; you will see potential threats or obstacles sooner, which gives more time to initiate a response. The driver should

develop the ability to look at least 600 meters ahead. This allows the operator to be alert for potentially dangerous situations, which will require some form of response. This may be an observation of brake lights on vehicles in front or it could be a cloud of dust or smoke from a crash 2km away. In any driving situation, evasive, high-speed or otherwise, information means survival and the sooner the driver acquires the information and can process it, the better the chances of survival and/or mission accomplishment.

WARNING: *If the operator's eyes settle on the rear of any vehicle ahead, they will subconsciously slow down, which wastes speed as well as time.*

As the driver approaches a vehicle to overtake, he/she should drift out wide to either side of the lane and look underneath the vehicle, because from a distance the shadow or even the wheels from a car directly in front of that vehicle will be visible. This is critical in overtaking in heavy traffic. High-speed overtaking in traffic is just plain dangerous if the driver can't identify a spot to slot into in front of the slow vehicle.

In an evasive or high-performance driving situation, the operator should always be looking for places to escape to which are safer than being involved in a high-speed crash. An example is the choice between driving over a concrete median strip rather than striking a spike strip or a three-vehicle roadblock. Negotiating the median strip will mean braking severely and then bouncing over the median, possibly damaging the vehicle's steering or suspension and then being forced to drive on the wrong side of the road until an exit can be found or a Handbrake Turn executed. Hitting the spike strip will mean almost instant loss of a good chunk of vehicle control and reaction times as the tyres shred down to the bare rims. Hitting the roadblock could mean being shot or badly injured in a collision while attempting to ram the blocking vehicle/s out of the way.

Reading the road

Concrete Road Surface:

Concrete is a supportive surface. When it is new, the surface is very abrasive and provides excellent traction. As it ages, concrete becomes less adherent and more conducive to hydro planning and skids if wet. Concrete is very light in colour, almost white when it is new. As it ages, the colour becomes darker as the rubber from tyres builds up on the concrete.

Asphalt Road Surface

Asphalt is a distributive surface. When it is new, the surface is slick and oily and not conducive to good traction. As it ages, the aggregate rock begins to surface as the oils are pushed down and away. This results in increased traction. New asphalt surfaces are dark, often black. As it ages, the colour lightens to grey.

Reading the surface of the roadway will allow the operator to anticipate changes in traction. This takes practice and discipline but can become second nature. A good rule of thumb is this:

THE LIGHTER THE COLOUR OF THE DRIVING SURFACE, THE BETTER TRACTION THERE WILL BE.

Night Driving Adjustments

Driving at night presents its own set of problems. Nearly everything in the road environment has been artificially enhanced for better visibility at night. Devices such as reflective paint and tape enhance road signs and markers. This often has the unfortunate result of tricking the driver into believing visibility is actually better than it is in natural daylight. The eye's night vision is nowhere near as effective as it is in daylight.

Without night vision equipment, the operator loses most of his/her secondary vision and the peripheral vision is severely limited. The driver must mentally make the adjustment for night driving and limit speed as far as is practicable. They need to remember to scan from side to side and not attempt to rely on peripheral vision. This will help to reduce surprise and make driving smoother.

Road Hazards

These can come in many forms. Some of the most common include animals, vehicle debris, potholes, etc. The operator should always attempt to locate the hazard visually in plenty of time to allow slowing and or maneuvering of the vehicle.

Sometimes a hazard presents itself with no warning. This is where the operator must combine sound decision-making with driving skill. It is not worth the potential damage to the operational vehicle to take extreme evasive action to avoid hitting a small animal. It is preferable for the operator to instead hit the animal and maintain control of the vehicle to allow completion of the mission.

When the operator determines that the safest course of action is to strike a hazard such as small animals, vehicle debris or pothole, he or she can utilize weight transfer techniques to successfully minimize damage to the vehicle and maintain positive control. When the hazard is spotted and the only option is to hit it, the operator should press the brakes as hard as possible. This will have the effect of shifting weight forward dramatically and "loading" the suspension components with energy. A split second prior to impact, the driver should release the brakes. This has the effect of allowing all the stored potential energy in the suspension system to rapidly release. Weight will automatically transfer to the rear of the vehicle, which will help to "bounce" the vehicle over the object.

Braking

The materials in brakes are typically manufactured to withstand approximately 650°F of heat. While they seem to be sufficient, there have been many times during vehicle testing that temperatures in excess of 1400°F have been recorded. This is more than twice what the system was engineered to withstand and as such, when temperatures of that magnitude begin to build, a degradation of braking effectiveness begins to occur.

There are two common types of braking system, drum brakes and disc brakes.

Drum brakes are an internal expanding system. As the brake components begin to heat up, the drum actually expands, causing the brake shoes to travel a greater distance. Drum brakes typically cool in about 20-30% of the drum while approximately 70-80% of the drum is involved in the heat exchange process. Drum brakes must be adjusted periodically. In order to adjust the brakes, the operator can back up and engage the brakes a few times. This will realign the shoe with the drum, making the brakes operate at their full capacity.

Disc brake systems are called an external expanding system. As the components heat up due to braking, the disc actually closes the distance the pads must travel to contact it.

Disc brakes are typically more efficient in managing heat. Only about 20% of the actual disc is involved in braking, while approximately 80% of the disc is being cooled by the vehicle's slipstream.

Anti-lock brake systems are designed as an emergency aid for the driver. They allow the tyres to continue to turn rather than lock and slide, giving the driver increased directional control.

Contact between the surfaces of the braking components generates heat due to friction. Friction must occur for braking to occur. Braking occurs when the heat energy created by the friction is dissipated throughout the brake disc or drum. When these components no longer exchange heat effectively, brake fade occurs.

At all times, you should treat the brakes gently Never stab or jam on the brakes. All braking should be done as smoothly and efficiently as the situation allows.

Cornering

The fastest route a driver can take through a corner is often called the "racing line". If the operator is able to identify and use the racing line at moderate speed, he or she will outrun a vehicle which travels at the same speed but takes an incorrect line. The speed at which the vehicle exits the corner is far more important than the speed at which the vehicle enters. If the car accelerates through the corner and exits correctly, it will have greater speed on any straight which may follow the corner.

Some important cornering terms which will be discussed are:

Braking Point:

The braking point is the point at which the operator begins to slow the vehicle enough to negotiate the corner.

The Entry Point:

The entry point is where the operator turns the steering wheel to begin the curve.

The Entrance:

The entrance is the path taken from the entry point to the apex.

Apex:

The apex in any turn is the point in which the vehicle's wheels are closest to the inside edge of the corner. By choosing a relatively late apex, the operator can exit a corner at a greater speed than if he or she had chosen a later one.

The Exit:

The exit is the path taken from the apex to the exit point.

The Exit Point

The exit point is the route out of the corner.

90° Corner

This is the most common type of corner in urban areas.

This corner is begun as far to the outside as possible. If there is traffic on the road, the operator will have to adjust the turn to compensate.

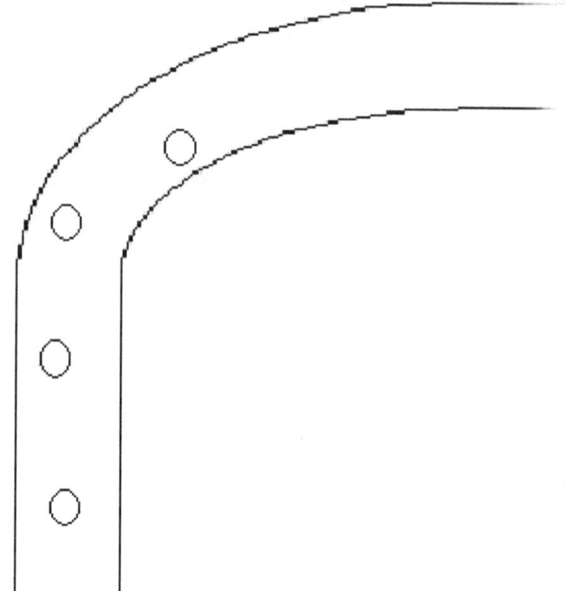

S-Turns

An S-Type turn is a series of corners in which the road winds in the shape of an "S". If the corners are sharp, the operator will need to alternate the racing line until through the "S". If the corner is gentle, it is possible to cut straight through the corners.

Constant Radius Corners

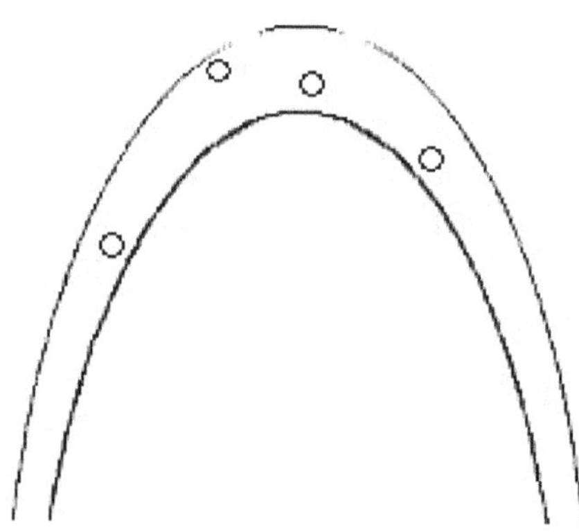

A constant radius turn also known as a hairpin. The racing line is similar to a 90 degree corner except that the angle of attack is more acute. It is important not to drive too fast on these turns to avoid skidding off the road.

Sequence of Events – suitable for all turns:

1. *As the operator approaches the corner, they brake and downshift while still traveling in a straight line. Then, as the vehicle enters the turn, the operator is able to concentrate fully on steering the vehicle through the corner. It is important to release the clutch before beginning the corner to avoid unbalancing the vehicle.*

2. *As soon as the vehicle reaches the Entry point, the operator steers the vehicle towards the apex. The operator maintains the vehicle's balance with a light pressure on the accelerator until the vehicle has successfully transitioned into the turn. The path from the entry point should be a smooth arc.*

3. *As the vehicle approaches the apex of the turn, the operator uses ocular driving to look ahead to the exit point and accelerates gently at the apex. The vehicle will then take the exit toward the exit point.*

4. *As the vehicle approaches the exit of the corner, the operator accelerates out of the corner and uses ocular driving to look ahead to the next turn or the straight.*

Skid control

Front Skids

Front Skids occur when the front end of the vehicles takes a wider path than desired. The drive force and the turning force do not balance. As per the laws of physics, the vehicle will attempt to travel in a straight line. In automotive terms, this condition is known as "understeer". In

simple terms, for whatever the reason, the front end of the vehicle has become unresponsive. Other terms that describe this condition of a vehicle include "tight", "pushing" and "plowing". In the corner example, the drive force (A), is equal to the turn force (B) and the result is a smooth line

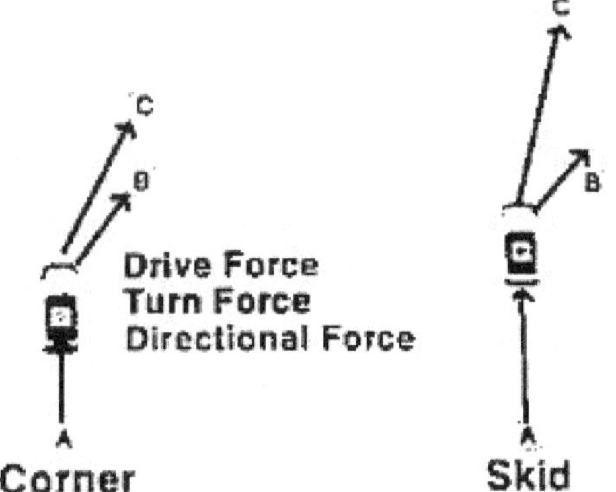

around the corner.

In the skid example, the drive force (A) has exceeded the turn force (B). The resulting directional force (C)

Correcting Front Skids:

1. Straighten out the steering wheel to allow the front tyres to regain rolling friction.

2. Turn back into the corner smoothly.

3. If you are on the accelerator, ease off. This will transfer weight to the front tyres.

4. If you are on the brakes, ease off enough to ensure they are not locked up.

Rear Skids

Rear skids occur when the rear of the vehicle takes a wider path than desired. In automotive terms, this is known as "oversteer". In simple terms, the rear of the vehicle has become unresponsive. Other terms include "loose" or "fishtailing".

The key to understanding rear skids is to examine the forces at work on the vehicle's rear tyres.

When a vehicle travels around a corner and forces are equal, the net result is a smooth corner. If the slide force exceeds the drive force, the vehicle will begin a rear skid. It is important to remember that a sliding tyre is faster than one that is turning, to the only thing the tyre can do is attempt to travel past the front of the vehicle, causing the rear of the vehicle to skid.

Correcting Rear Skids:

1. Straighten the steering wheel quickly but smoothly

2. If you are on the accelerator, ease off smoothly. This will minimize weight transfer to the front of the vehicle, which will

   tend to make the skid worse.

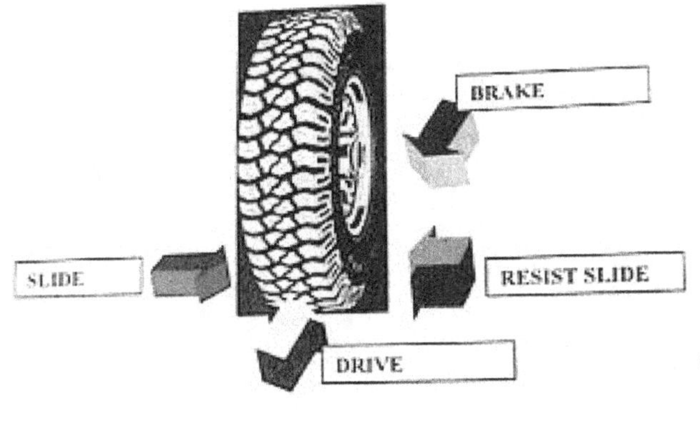

3. If you are on the brakes, ease of to transfer weight to the sliding tyres.

General Skid Control:

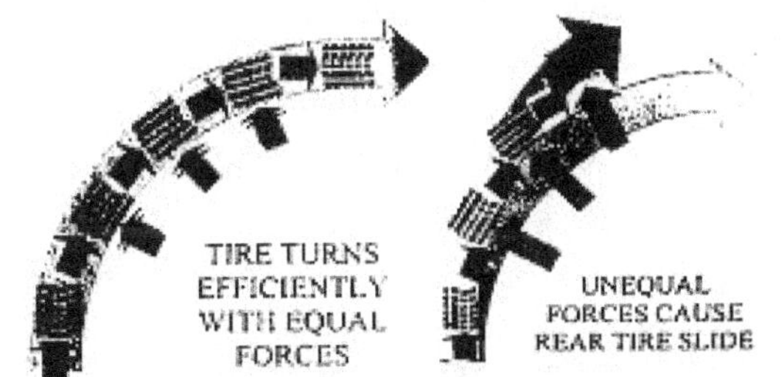

IN ANY SKID OR SLIDE, TRY

TO DO <u>LESS</u> OF WHATEVER

YOU DID TO CREATE THE

PROBLEM – AND DO IT

SMOOTHLY.

Threshold braking

Threshold braking is the most efficient method to conduct an emergency stop. It is defined as maximum pressure applied to the brake pedal, just short of locking up the wheels. When the vehicle is equipped with an ABS (anti-lock) system, the threshold occurs at the point of ABS engagement.

As heat builds up in the braking system, the brake's effectiveness will decrease. The operator should try to keep the heel of his/her braking foot firmly planted on the floorboard of the vehicle.

Double-declutch

Double-declutch is a driving technique which is actually more difficult to describe than to execute. The purpose of the double-declutch is to match the speed of the engine to the speed of the rotating parts of the gearbox for the gear the operator wishes to select. Once the speeds are matched, the gear will engage smoothly. If the speeds are not matched, the gears will grate as they come into mesh. A modern synchromesh gearbox accomplishes this automatically, which negates the need for double-declutching.

To perform a double-declutch:,

1. the clutch is pressed and the gearbox shifted into neutral.

2. The clutch is released, the throttle is "blipped" which applies power to the disengaged gearbox, speeding it up internally.

3. The clutch is pressed for a second time and the gear lever smoothly shifted into the desired gear.

4. The clutch is released again and the vehicle accelerates in the new gear.

This operation is suitable for a down-change. For an up-change, it is usually sufficient to allow the gear lever to rest momentarily in neutral with no throttle applied before shifting into a higher gear. The whole procedure can take no more than a fraction of a second with practice.

The double-declutch is used in maneuvers such as the handbrake turn.

Mastering the double-declutch is essential for high-performance driving.

Heel-and-toe

Heel-and-Toe is a driving techniques used in high-performance and evasive driving. It involves operating the brake pedal and the accelerator pedal simultaneously with the right foot and has the effect of freeing up the left foot for techniques such as the double-declutch or otherwise changing gear while braking heavily.

CHAPTER 4

EVASIVE DRIVING

Once you recognize an attack is occurring, decisions must be made immediately. If the scenario is an armed attack or assassination attempt, get out of the kill zone. Typically potential adversaries have a relatively narrow window of time and may have restricted fields of fire due to obstacles in their path. Once you exit the kill zone, non-state actors such as organized criminals and terrorists will rarely pursue you since they must begin their own escape and evasion plan. Officially sanctioned adversaries such as paramilitary or intelligence teams, police, Special Forces, etc. will press home their intentions and the only way the operator will foil such an attack is to evade their way through it.

Attack Recognition

If terrorists succeed in surveilling you and plan an attack, the next place to foil their efforts is to recognize their intentions and prepare to escape. Recognizing an attack scenario is difficult. Often what may appear to be an attack is more likely to be innocent circumstances. However, alertness and willingness to act are the keys to surviving a genuine attack scenario. The following are typical abnormal situations:

- Individuals who appear to be excessively nervous and seem out of place by dress or mannerisms.

- Individuals wearing unusually long or heavy clothing for the environment.

- Individuals who appear to be acting as lookouts along your route of travel.

- Staged auto or bike accident in your path.

- Vehicles that hit your car from the front or rear.

- Unusual detours, vehicle roadblocks, cones, or other barriers. Be prepared to escape by going around the obstacle or ramming it.

- Vehicles traveling with items protruding from side doors or vans traveling with side doors open.

- Disabled vehicles, hitchhikers, or distressed "accident victims" seeking your assistance are commonly employed traps.
- A flagman, workman, or fake police or government checkpoint stopping your car at an isolated or otherwise suspicious place.

- Sudden unusual activity or the unexplained absence of local civilians.

- Gunfire

Evasive Maneuvers

Handbrake Turn

Only useful in a rear-wheel drive vehicle, the purpose of a Handbrake Turn is to change direction 180 degrees in an emergency. It allows the operator to rapidly reverse the direction of travel without stopping and within the confines of a two-lane road. The usual use of the Handbrake Turn is to evade vehicle checkpoints or roadblocks and to frustrate high-speed pursuit.

Note: The use of the Handbrake Turn in an all-terrain 4WD or sports utility vehicle is extremely dangerous. A rollover is highly likely due to the high center of gravity of these vehicles. Rollover in a standard sedan is also possible if the vehicle encounters the curb or other obstacles such as speed humps while executing the Handbrake Turn. The handbrake turn is most effective in a rear-wheel drive vehicle. See the "Left Foot Braking" Section for an overview of similar maneuvers preformed in a front wheel drive vehicle.

The Handbrake Turn is easier to execute in vehicles with an automatic transmission and a hand emergency brake. It is possible to execute the Handbrake Turn in a vehicle with a manual transmission, however more steps are involved. Handbrake Turns in a manual transmission vehicle will require more practice than with an automatic transmission, but the end result is a faster turn with more positive control.

For clarity, the exact procedure for both transmission types is described below.

Automatic Transmission:

-     Accelerate to between 45-50 km
2. Remove your foot from the accelerator Place your palm flat on the bottom center of the steering wheel and swing it hard and fast around one and a half times. At this point it is important to lean against the turn to prevent a rollover.

3. When the vehicle is at approximately 90 degrees to the original line of travel, rapidly shift the automatic transmission into a lower gear then simultaneously release the handbrake, depress the accelerator pedal and straighten the steering wheel.

4. Rapidly accelerate forward in the opposite direction to the original line of travel.

Manual Transmission:

1. Accelerate to between 65-65 km/h

2. Place your palm flat on the bottom center of the steering wheel and swing it hard and fast around one and a half times. At this point it is important to lean against the turn to prevent a rollover.

3. As the nose of the vehicle dips sharply and lunges to the right, the rear of the vehicle will begin to slide out to the left. Keeping the power on, reach down for the handbrake.

4. As soon as the vehicle is fully committed to the skid, snap up the handbrake. This will rapidly whip the vehicle around and will reduce the length of the skid.

WARNING: *It is extremely important not to touch the brake pedal during this maneuver to prevent the wheels from locking up.*

5. At this point, the vehicle will be sliding backwards down the road and decelerating rapidly. Rapidly double-declutch and shift into first gear, apply the power so that the wheels will start spinning and then grab before the vehicle comes to a halt.

6. Moving up through the gears, rapidly accelerate forward in the opposite direction to the original line of travel.

The J-Turn

The J-Turn is basically a Handbrake Turn performed while driving in reverse, but without using the handbrake. This maneuver is useful if the operator unexpectedly drives into an ambush or is forced to stop at a vehicle checkpoint. The technique allows the vehicle to change direction 180 degrees within the confines of a two-lane road. The operator rapidly backs out of the danger zone, turns and drives off in the opposite direction.

Note: The use of the J-Turn in an all-terrain 4WD or sports utility vehicle is extremely dangerous. A rollover is highly likely due to the high center of gravity of these vehicles. Rollover in a standard sedan is also possible if the vehicle encounters the curb or other obstacles such as speed humps while executing the J-Turn.

Like the Handbrake Turn, the J-Turn is easier to execute in vehicles with an automatic transmission. It is possible to execute the J-Turn in a vehicle with a manual transmission, however more steps are involved. J-Turns in a manual transmission vehicle will require more practice than with an automatic transmission, but the end result is a faster turn with more positive control.

For clarity, the exact procedure for both transmission types is described below.

Automatic Transmission:

1. Draw to a halt while simultaneously checking the rear-vision mirrors for any obstructions or adversaries attempting a box-in maneuver.

2. Shift into reverse Accelerate rapidly and steer straight back at approximately 40-50km/h.

3. Remove your foot from the accelerator and swing the steering wheel all the way to right as far as possible.

WARNING: *It is extremely important not to touch the brake pedal during this maneuver to prevent the wheels from locking up. Braking is unnecessary as the front wheels will steer the nose around, negating the need for braking.*

4. When the vehicle has turned 90 degrees, hit the accelerator and straighten the steering wheel.

5. Rapidly accelerate forward in the opposite direction to the original line of travel.

Manual Transmission:

1. Draw to a halt while simultaneously checking the rear-vision mirrors for any obstructions or adversaries attempting a box-in maneuver.
2. Shift into reverse Accelerate rapidly and steer straight back at approximately 40-50km/h.

3. Place your palm flat on the bottom center of the steering wheel and swing it hard and fast around one and a half times. At this point it is important to lean against the turn to prevent a rollover.

4. As the vehicle swings into line, rapidly double-declutch and shift into first gear, apply the power so that the wheels will start spinning and then grab before the vehicle comes to a halt.

5. Moving up through the gears, rapidly accelerate forward in the opposite direction to the original line of travel.

Left Foot Braking

Left foot braking is a technique that allows a front-wheel drive vehicle to efficiently execute a Handbrake Turn-type maneuver. It involves locking the rear wheels with the foot brake. As the right foot must be free to operate the accelerator during this maneuver, the left foot is used to apply the brake. The vehicle is balanced using engine power by use of the accelerator pedal.

Manual Transmission:

1. Accelerate to between 65-65 km/h

2. Place your palm flat on the bottom center of the steering wheel and swing it hard and fast around one and a half times. At this point it is important to lean against the turn to prevent a rollover.

3. As the nose of the vehicle dips sharply and lunges to the right, the rear of the vehicle will begin to slide out to the left.

4. As soon as the vehicle is fully committed to the skid, apply full pressure to the brake pedal with the left foot.. This will rapidly whip the vehicle around and will reduce the length of the skid.

5. At this point, the vehicle will be sliding backwards down the road and decelerating rapidly. Release the brake pedal and rapidly double-declutch and shift into first gear, apply the power so that the wheels will start spinning and then grab before the vehicle comes to a halt.

6. Moving up through the gears, rapidly accelerate forward in the opposite direction to the original line of travel.

Opposite Lock

Opposite lock is a colloquial term used to mean the deliberate use of oversteer to turn a vehicle rapidly without losing momentum. It is typified by the classic rally driving style where a car appears to travel around a tight bend sideways.

The term "opposite lock" refers to the position of the steering wheel during the maneuver, which is turned in the opposite direction to the bend.

The technique is only useful for rear-wheel drive vehicles and works best on loose surfaces where the friction between the tyres and the road is not to high.

1. Before entry to the bend, the vehicle is turned towards the bend slightly, but quickly, so as to cause a rotating motion that induces the rear of the vehicle to slide outwards.

2. The vehicle accelerates, which applies further sideways movement. At the same time, opposite lock steering is applied to keep the car on the desired course.

3.   As the vehicle reaches the bend it will have already turned through most of the required angle, traveling sideways and losing some speed as a result. A smooth application of power at this point will accelerate the vehicle into the bend and then through it, gradually removing the sideways component.

Dealing With Barricades

Barricades can include hasty vehicle checkpoints, spike strips, felled trees, concrete barriers, etc. Deliberate barricades are generally set up on blind corners to reduce the reaction time of the driver.

Hasty and deliberate barricades are often covered by weapons fire, which means that there is a high probability of the operator and any passengers being hit by hostile fire.

Upon detecting the barricade, the operator must rapidly deduce the probability of being able to either steer around, ram, or retreat from the barricade.

Steering Around

Steering around an obstacle that extends across a single lane is relatively easy to avoid. All the operator must do is to swerve into the clear lane and pass the obstacle. If the obstacle extends across all lanes, then steering around is a less preferred method as it means leaving the roadway.

If it is necessary to steer off the roadway while avoiding an obstacle, the driver must slow to a safer speed and visually verify that the chosen path doesn't contain ditches or other obstacles. The average non-modified civilian vehicle is capable of pushing through rough terrain, light vegetation and wire fences. The dangers with this method are being bogged down in muddy conditions, striking an unseen log, rock or ditch and drawing hostile fire.

If a kerb or gutter is encountered, it is possible to negotiate at speed. The kerb must be struck at a 45 degree angle to ensure that the steering, oil reservoir, wheel and differential are not damaged.

Ramming

It is possible to ram through a barricade consisting of single or double vehicles. The operator must wear a seatbelt and be prepared for the fact that the vehicle may be damaged an evasion on foot will be necessary. An added hazard is that it is entirely likely that the barricade will be covered by hostile fire from the adversary's barricade team as well as a security element positioned before or after the barricade. It is for the above reasons that ramming is generally the method of last resort.

Single Vehicle Barricades

After the situation has been evaluated and the decision made to ram through the barricade, the operator should slow down as he or she approaches the barricade. This will give the adversary the impression that the vehicle will stop. The operator should then ensure the vehicle is in a low gear and accelerate sharply. The operator should hit the chosen target area at an angle and keep the accelerator fully depressed through the manoeuvre. The speed at impact should be between 30-50km/h. Once through, the operator should accelerate forward as fast as the vehicle will travel, even if badly damaged. Studies have shown that even a badly damaged vehicle can travel a considerable distance, which will give the operator more options.

Double Vehicle Barricades

A double vehicle barricade will usually consist of two vehicles parked in a line extending across both lanes of the roadway. Using the subterfuge method described above, the easiest way to breach such a barricade is to strike in between the vehicles, forcing them apart.

The preferred target area is the rear of the stationary target vehicle as it is lighter than the front of the vehicle which contains the engine and is thus heavier. The target vehicle should be struck at a point just forward of the rear wheel arch. If the rear of the target vehicle is unavailable for ramming, the front may be struck, once again just forward the wheel arch.

Retreating from the Barricade.

If the barricade is detected and evaluated in time, the best method is to execute a handbrake turn or left foot braking before coming into effective range of hostile fire.

If the barricade is not detected until the operator is almost on top of it, the best method of retreat is to slow to a stop, then suddenly execute a j-turn. If there is no room for a J-turn, simply reversing out of the danger area or kill zone at high speed is a viable option.

Retreat is the most preferred method of dealing with barricades as it is the safest method

CHAPTER 5

TACTICAL VEHICLE INTERDICTION

In some cases, the objective of the operation may be to recover friendly or kill/snatch threat personnel. While performing these tasks against a vehicle-mobile adversary may not be the method of choice, it is often easier than a full-scale assault on a heavily guarded and/or politically sensitive building or compound. Tactical Vehicle Interdiction (or TVI) is defined simply as forcing a vehicle to halt or preventing it from escaping in order to execute an operational objective.

Stopping several tons of moving metal is not an easy task. In the paragraphs below, the operator will be exposed to the basic concepts and techniques of Tactical Vehicle Interception. As with most operations of this type, it is infinitely simpler to kill or destroy a vehicle and the personnel operating or traveling in it if it is halted rather than on the move. There are two main categories of TVI: Static TVI and Mobile TVI.

Static Vehicle Interdiction

Static Vehicle Interdiction involves securing a static vehicle and its contents and preventing it from escaping. The key to a successful Static TVI is attacking the objective while it is halted. This can mean setting up planned or hasty roadblocks, vehicle checkpoints using subterfuge, conventional ambush techniques, sabotage or explosive interdiction. Operational and environmental characteristics of the target and its environment will determine which method is used.

Road Blocks

The easiest and most effective way of interdicting a static vehicle is by the use of a hasty roadblock. A roadblock is a covert technique that is meant to simply destroy or snatch their target and disappear. The roadblock will generally consist of two or more vehicles as well as two armed "stop" groups positioned immediately before and after the roadblock position. The roadblock is best situated just after a blind corner on a single or two-lane road.

Good intelligence on the target vehicle's direction, speed and likely destination are crucial when attempting any form of tactical vehicle interception. This is provided by a small vehicle surveillance team who will guide the roadblock group to the likely roadblock position. It is also important that the roadblock group have an excellent understanding of the layout of the local roads as well as have previously reconnoitered suitable roadblock positions.

Once it is confirmed that the target vehicle is heading towards the roadblock group, it occupies the pre-selected roadblock position on that route. In a two-vehicle roadblock, the blocking vehicles are parked nose-to-tail across both lanes of traffic. If available, rocks, metal pipes, tree trunks or other obstacles should be placed in position on either side of the roadblock. These obstacles should be placed slightly off center in relation to the blocking vehicles to ensure that if the operation is compromised or the target is able to mount an effective counter-attack, the blocking vehicles will be able to escape without the threat of being caught up in their own obstacles.

The security or "stop" groups can consist of one operator or several. Their sole purpose is to stop the target vehicle if it is able to breach the

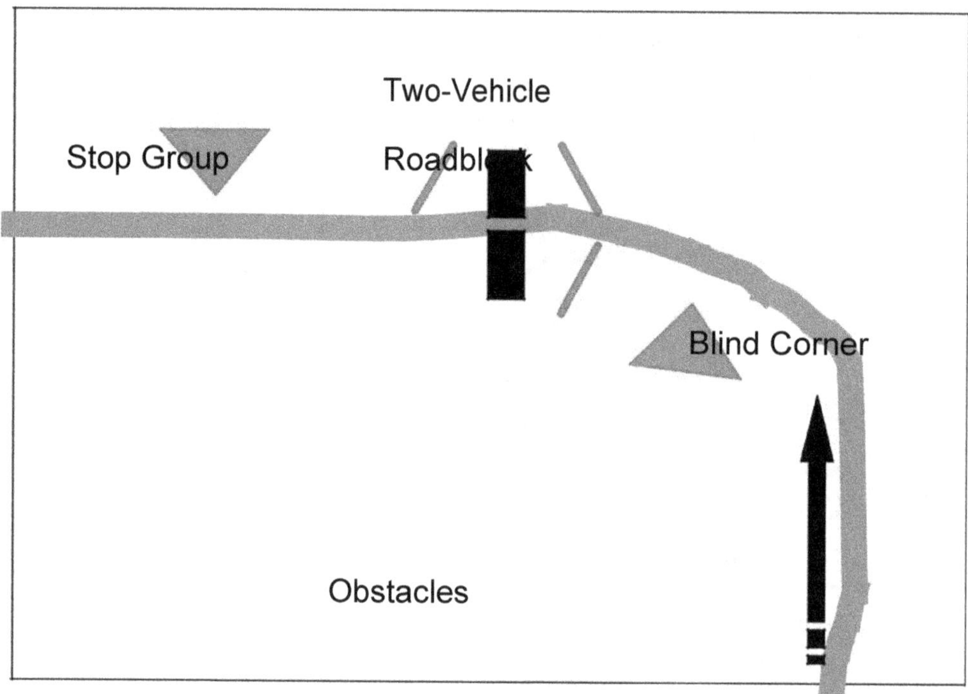

Target Vehicle Direction of Travel

roadblock or otherwise evade it. They are placed immediately before and after the roadblock and are equipped with radio communications and heavier weapons. In a three-man stop group, two operators will be armed with assault rifles such as M4s or AK-series rifles. The third operator will be armed with a shotgun loaded with rifled lead slugs. While a small-calibre assault rifle will definitely stop an escaping vehicle, it is unlikely that it will do so immediately. It may take several 30-round magazines to stop the vehicle, which will have by then traveled at least several hundred meters. This gives the threat personnel inside the vehicle a good chance to escape the roadblock on foot if they are uninjured. The shotgun-armed operator can instantly shred a moving vehicle's tyres; punch large holes through vehicle body panels and even penetrate armored glass or cave in armored windows.

The key to a successful roadblock is to instantly and violently kill, capture or rescue the target as soon as the vehicle stops.

If the vehicle attempts a handbrake or j turn before the roadblock, the stop group will interdict it, thereby avoiding a lengthy pursuit. If the vehicle attempts to ram the blocking vehicles out of the way, the road blocking team must be certain that the vehicle will not be able to penetrate the barrier, by using heavy chains between the tow points on the vehicles or packing the trunk of each vehicle with lead or concrete blocks to present a harder target. The well-sited hidden or overt obstacles mentioned previously will stop a target attempting to go around the roadblock and if not, it will be slowed enough that the second stop group will have time to effectively interdict the vehicle with weapons fire.

Vehicle Checkpoints

The Vehicle Checkpoint (VCP) is commonly used by law enforcement, customs, security and military forces throughout the world. It is an overt roadblock where a random sample of vehicles are stopped and the driver's credentials scrutinized and or the vehicle searched for contraband, fugitives, etc. It would be unwise for a team of paramilitary operators on a deniable operation in a hostile or neutral country to ask for the cooperation of local law enforcement in order to assassinate a known terrorist. However, the technique can be utilized by using subterfuge and camouflage. Good logistics and of course, intelligence, are the keys to a covert/overt VCP.

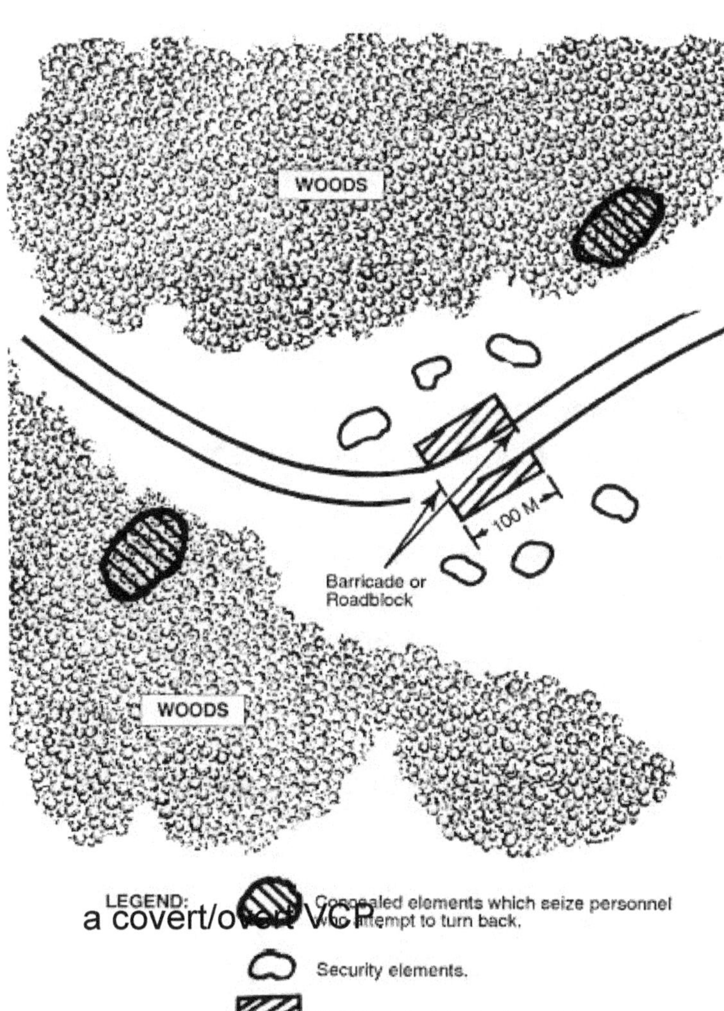

LEGEND:

Concealed elements which seize personnel who attempt to turn back.

Security elements.

Vehicle and personnel inspection areas.

The team obtains uniforms and equipment of local security or military forces and establishes a genuine-looking VCP on a route that the target vehicle is known to be traveling along. As with a hasty roadblock, the VCP team is supported by a surveillance element and at least two stop groups. The VCP is sited in an area where it is unlikely that the genuine security or military forces will travel, but which the target will transit. The VCP is established with road construction barriers and official-looking police vehicles complete with flashers.

Until the target arrives, civilian vehicles are randomly stopped and scrutinized, then sent on their way. When the surveillance team reports that the target is on his way, the "Officers" manning the VCP randomly

select the target vehicle. Once the vehicle is stopped, the passengers are subjected to license and vehicle scrutiny. Due to an irregularity or other such official "problem", the passengers are arrested and placed into one of the police vehicles. The VCP is then dismantled and the prisoners may be taken to an accommodation address for interrogation or disposal.

Civilians who have seen the VCP will not intervene in the arrest as long as the VCP and the police themselves appear and act authentic.

Major points to consider when establishing VCPs:

1. Concealment - Position VCPs so they cannot be seen from long distances. Sharp bends or dips in a road provide ideal concealment.

2. Security - Position stop groups before and after the VCP to deal with a fleeing target vehicle. For operational security and deniability reasons, VCP personnel should also be armed with weapons and equipment native to the local area's police or security forces.

3. Construction & Layout - Set up the VCP so it is visible to traffic flow once there is no egress except through the VCP.

Explosive Interdiction

Explosive Interdiction means disabling or destroying a vehicle through

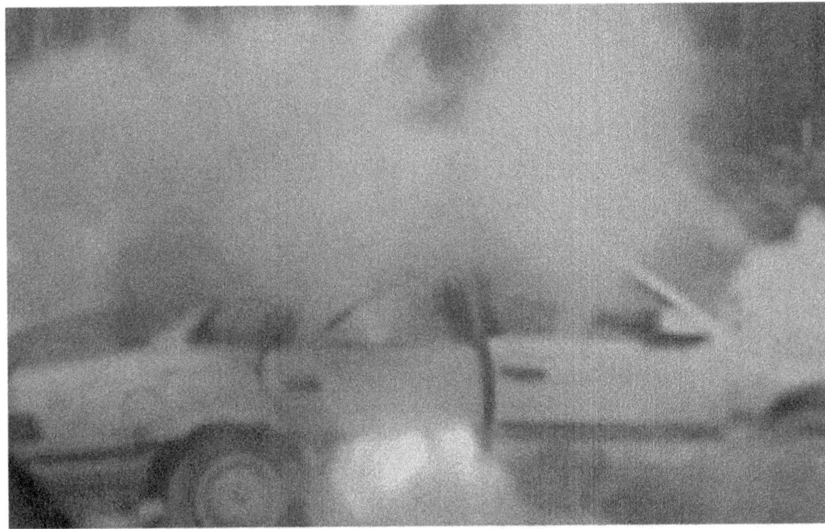

the use of mines, booby traps, aircraft delivered munitions or anti-tank weapons. For the purposes of this section, explosive interdiction refers to under-car booby traps (or UCBTs) placed on a vehicle while it is parked or otherwise static.

This method of static vehicle interdiction requires good intelligence as to where the vehicle is routinely parked as well as any security measures in the area such as guards, video cameras or even expedient security measures such as a dusty vehicle, or clear tape strips placed on window and door seals. The best way to obtain such intelligence is through covert surveillance.

Once the required intelligence has been obtained, a reconnaissance must be made to determine the security measures used on the vehicle such as the improvised measures described above or car alarms, etc. If the vehicle is garaged, a covert methods of entry team may be required to surreptitiously enter the garage and the vehicle.

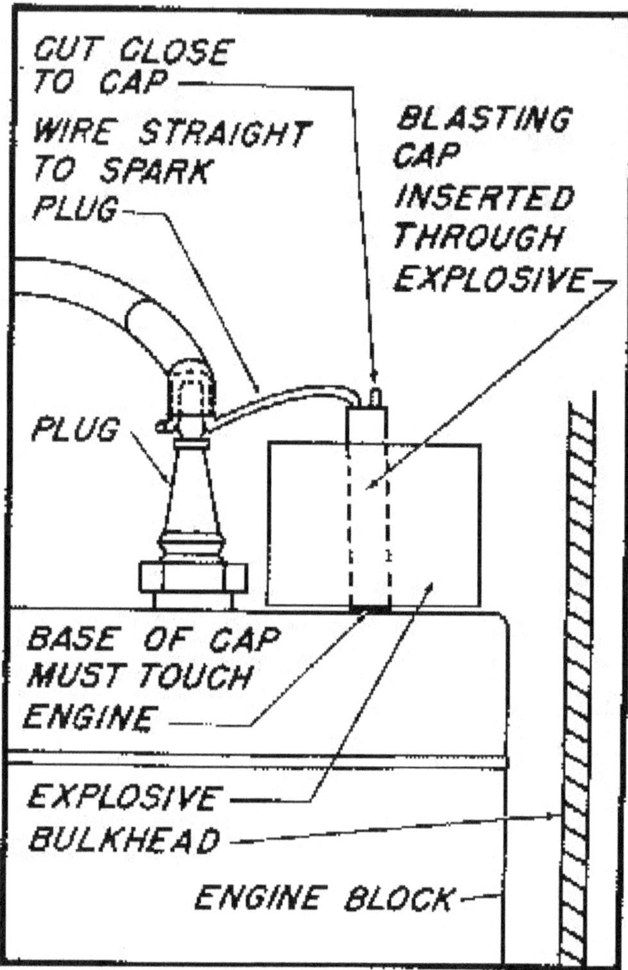

Vehicle Booby Trap

Due to the fact that the most common UCBT detection method uses an under-vehicle search mirror, the team should avoid placing the UCBT actually under the vehicle unless it is concealed behind vehicle components such as a spare wheel, differential or suspension system. Ideally, the UCBT should be placed in the interior of the vehicle or in the engine bay. This will generally require defeating vehicle locks or security systems. Further information on this can be found in the "Tactical Vehicle Commandeering" section of this manual.

The simplest UCBT consists of a firing wire, a blasting cap and a main charge placed in the engine bay and wired to detonate when the engine is started. This method uses the engine rocker cover and the spark plug as the firing system. It will not initiate until the ignition is switched all the way. It is important to snip off one of the blasting cap lead wires and wire the other to the spark plug as well as ensuring that the bottom of the blasting cap is touching the engine. See the accompanying diagram for more information. A difficult aspect of this technique is concealing the device, as the bottom of the

blasting cap must be

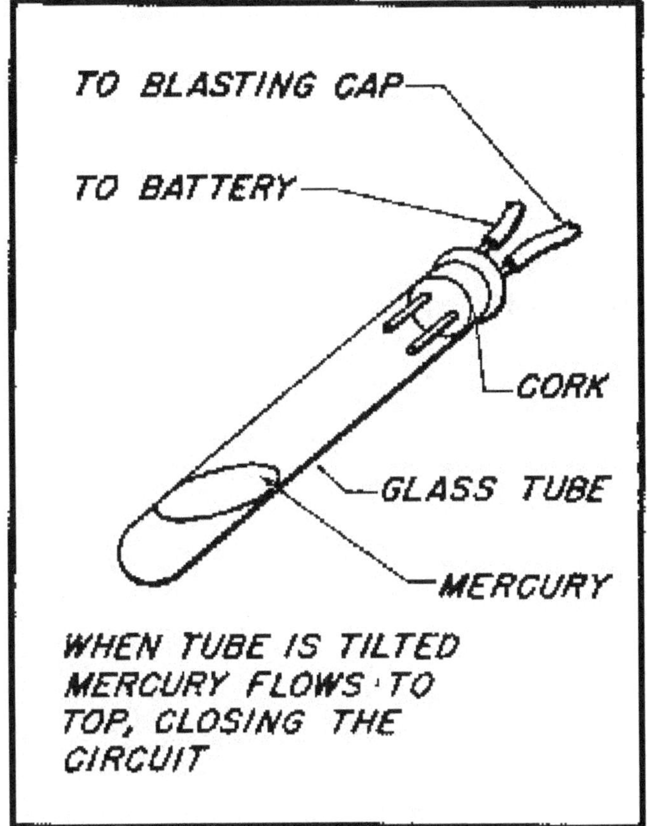

Electric Tilting Mercury Switch

contacting the rocker cover or engine block. Fixing the device to a dirty or oily engine will also cause problems with the device failing to adhere in place.

Other methods include the mercury switch and pressure switch methods. The beauty of these methods is that they are self contained and the mercury switch device need not even be placed inside the vehicle. The mercury switch is movement activated (see diagram). When the vehicle pitches while going up or down an incline, the mercury flows to the contacts, completing the circuit and detonating the device. It may be placed inside the vehicle or inside fenders, bumpers or nudge bars.

Other good places include:

- In air filter
- In false heater hose
- In windshield washer tank
- On top of gas tank (suspended or concealed in compartment)
- Under rocker panels
- Tied to axles
- In tail pipe
- In insulation under hood
- Under chrome
- Inside trunk lids
- Inside tubing on roof racks
- Inside tubing of surfboard or ski rack
- Taped behind bumper
- Attached to frame of car
- Behind headlights and taillights
- In fuse box
- Under false bottom of trunk beds
- Under front seat
- Under back seat
- Within vents (air and heater)
- Within door
- Within upholstery
- Behind instrumental panel

- ○ Under ornamental objects on dashboard

- ○ Inside floor consoles

- ○ Within arm rests

Vehicle Sabotage

There are two main reasons that the operator would sabotage a target vehicle. These are to prevent the vehicle from leaving the place where it is parked in order to affect a personnel snatch or rescue or to cause the vehicle to malfunction and wreck.

The simplest way to immobilize a vehicle is to simply let the air out of one or more tyres. This will cause the driver to change the wheel on the spot, force the driver to arrange alternate transport or call for assistance from an auto club. Other ways include jimmying open the fuel filler cover with a wooden wedge and introducing a large amount of ground cork into the fuel tank to clog the fuel filter, deactivating the vehicle's battery with alka-seltzer or baking soda or simply pouring a gallon of water into the fuel tank.

To cause the vehicle to malfunction, the simplest way is to cut the tyres to blow. This involves scoring the inside tyre wall with a sharp blade so that if the vehicle corners heavily, the tyre will blow out causing the vehicle to crash. If the team is overtly pursuing the target vehicle and causing the driver to undertake evasive maneuvers, this technique is even more effective. Cutting part way through the vehicle's brake lines to gradually depressurize them will have a similar effect.

The most effective method of vehicle sabotage is to place a large split-shot lead sinker on the vehicle's accelerator cable. The cable is extended fully and the sinker crimped around it. When the driver of the target vehicle applies a certain amount of pressure to the accelerator pedal, the throttle will stick open, which will cause an accident unless the driver is quick enough to put the vehicle into neutral and stop. Either way, the vehicle will be immobilized and it will be away from the target's compound or residence. To make these techniques more effective, the operator or CME team should use two or more at the same time. If the target vehicle's brakes fail at the same time as the throttle is stuck open, the vehicle will crash, giving the team an opportunity to move in while the target is immobilized, possibly injured and away from his base.

Mobile Vehicle Interdiction

Mobile TVI means stopping and/or disabling a moving vehicle, often at high speeds. This can be done with another vehicle or from a static position. Depending upon the reason for wanting the vehicle halted, it may be possible to disable or destroy the vehicle using the methods outlined below.

Precision Immobilization Technique

The precision immobilization technique (or PIT) is an offensive vehicle attack designed to cause an adversary to lose control of his vehicle. Originally developed by US intelligence and military units for stopping target vehicles, the PIT is such a successful method of mobile vehicle interdiction that it is used by law enforcement agencies to resolve high-speed pursuit situations.

Although a vehicle with specially reinforced bumpers should be used for this technique, any vehicle of either a similar or larger size than the target vehicle may be used. It is important to realize that under some circumstances, the vehicle performing the PIT may also become damaged or inoperable. It is for this reason that at least one back-up vehicle should follow the Interdiction team to provide transport, fire support and escape in the event of major vehicle damage.

The PIT is essentially a precision ramming technique which is best used with the element of surprise firmly in the operator's favor. Although the PIT is most effective on a bend or corner, it may be used on a straight stretch of road so long as the vehicle has the necessary power and speed.

PIT execution (*note: in the accompanying diagrams, the target vehicle is denoted by the red rectangular shape while the PIT vehicle is denoted by the blue rectangular shape*):

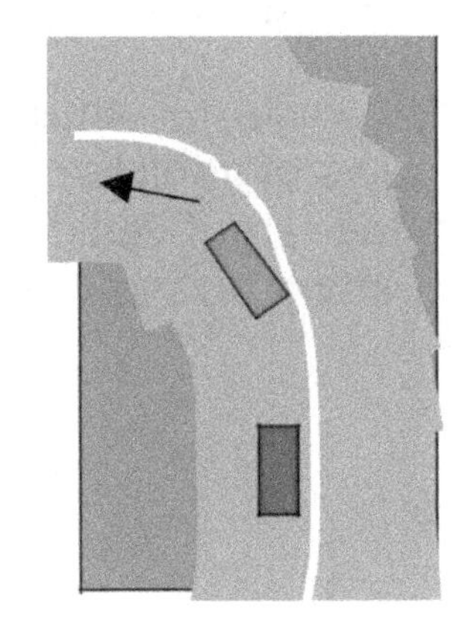

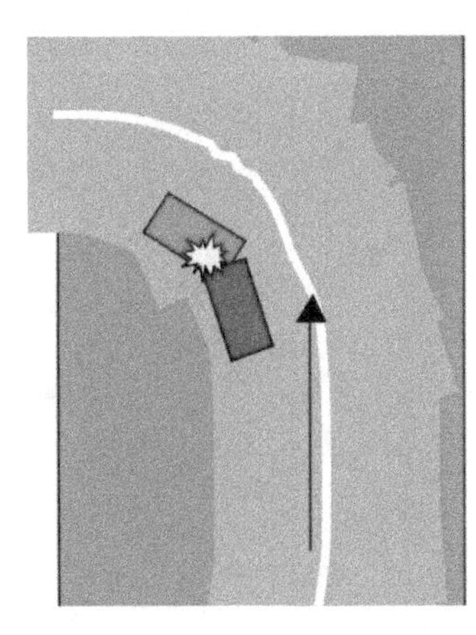

1.

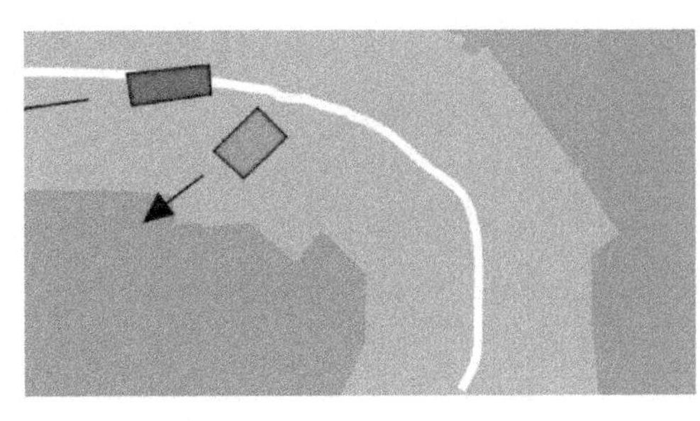

1.   While following or pursuing the target vehicle, wait for a
        bend or corner in the road.

2.   Heavily accelerate until the PIT vehicle is 20-45 km/h faster than the target
vehicle, and ram the target vehicle's rear corner

3.   The target vehicle will enter a spin and lose control. This occurs
        because the laws of vehicle dynamics decree that once the tyres regain
        their traction, the target vehicle will head in the direction in which the
        wheels are pointing. In this case, that means off the road.

CHAPTER 6

TACTICAL VEHICLE COMMANDEERING

Tactical vehicle commandeering is the seizure or theft of a non-attributable vehicle for operational purposes. There may be times when either by misfortune or design, the operator must procure his or her own means of transport without external support. Generally this will entail the theft of a vehicle through covert or overt means.

The methods detailed in this chapter are fundamentally the same as those used by professional car thieves. Most vehicle commandeering can be performed with inexpensive or easily-improvised tools such as slide-hammers, spark plugs, coat hanger wire, wooden wedges and plastic packing strapping.

Due to the fact that commandeered vehicles are more of a threat to security than vehicles sourced through regular channels, tactical vehicle commandeering must be considered a method of last resort.

This chapter will instruct the operator in methods used to select, enter and drive away common cars and motorcycle types. These methods should not be practiced without the aid of a qualified Tactical Vehicle Operations Instructor and due to their sensitive nature, the methods should not be disseminated to personnel without a direct need to know.

Vehicle Types and Selection

For most operations, an anonymous-looking vehicle with plenty of power is all that is required. Older six-to-eight cylinder cars fit this bill almost exactly. They generally lack the sophisticated security systems of modern types and have the horsepower to get the operator out of most threatening situations. In addition, older vehicles are more solidly made which means that unlike a newer "plastic" car with finely engineered crumple zones, the operator will probably not find the vehicle disabled whilst performing ramming techniques.

Choosing an older vehicle will help to reduce the major threat of any tactical vehicle commandeering operation – will the local authorities spend more time/resources looking for the stolen 2004 model Audi Quattro or the 1977 model Jaguar?

<u>Vehicle Selection Checklist:</u>Sedan.

- Sedans are the most common vehicle types on the world's roads.

- At least a six-cylinder engine

- Reliable front end and shocks – this generally means older European models such as BMWs, Volvos, Audis, Mercedes or Jaguars

- Simple security measures to defeat

o Four doors – if the whole team is traveling in a vehicle and there is an emergency, having to climb out of a two-seater could be fatal.

o Avoid "Classic" or "Flashy" vehicles. The object is to remain inconspicuous if not anonymous.

Vehicle Entry

Obviously, you can't procure a vehicle if you can't get into it. To gain entry to the vehicle you need to open the door or break a window. Below you will find descriptions of techniques for gaining entry to a secured vehicle, albeit a vehicle without a security alarm system. Methods for dealing with alarm systems are covered later in this chapter.

Just remember that these methods are usually much quicker, and easier than actually trying to pick the lock.

The most common entry areas is the Wing, or Vent Window. Or, in most of the newer models, The Rubber weather strip. You will need some special tools for this. The Curve, and the length of the tools are very important to work correctly.

The tool you decide to use should first be lubricated with a glycerine based hand or body lotion, or hand cleaner before you insert it through the weatherstripping. It makes the tool work much easier and free, and it also helps to prevent scarring, tearing, or any other kind of damage to the weatherstripping.

To open most front wing windows, get the lever latch tool, insert it though the weatherstripping between the wing window, and the window trim. Manipulate the tool by controlling the depth of penetration along the curve. While you are doing this, use a kind of Rocking Action to move the window lock into the Unlocked position.

Another type of Wing Window Lock has a lever latch with a Plunger at the pivot of the latch. The plunger deadlocks the latch against rotation

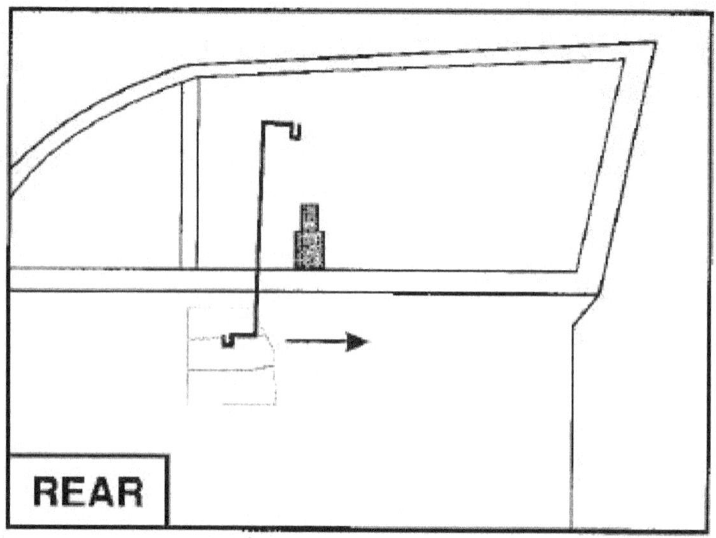

unless the plunger is first pushed in and held until the initial stage of rotation has been accomplished. This requires another tool being inserted though the weatherstripping and the door window to depress the plunger and hold it in that position while the other tool is used to rotate the latch. Usually, the tool used for depressing the deadlocking plunger has a slight curve at the tip.

1. Wedge the window in the center of door.
2. Insert the No. 95 and lower tool onto the upper linkage rod.
3. Twist tool to bite onto the upper linkage rod and push tool towards the front of vehicle to unlock door.

NOTE: No. 95 is a basic bent coathanger

Another way of access would be when the door window is fully raised and the door is locked. Take a bent wire, and using it on the locking mechanism. Tripping of the lock mechanism may often be done by pulling up on the wire. Once the tip of the wire has been positioned under the lock linkage. At other times, the bent tip of the wire must be pulled up against the linkage and then rotated to trip the locking mechanism. If you have practice at this, you will get the feel of what is required to open the door.

Vehicles using a Rocker type of locking mechanism can be tripped using a thin piece of flat spring steel stock. First, coat the tool with a hand lotion as said before. Insert the tool next to the glass or between the weather stripping and the metal of the door. Feel for the lock linkage with the notched end of the tool. Then move the linkage up and down until the lock moves into the Unlocked position.

Through the firewall, reaching the door locks with a long stiff wire to push out the lock button into the unlocked position also works.

Since automobile door locks on most newer models are normally held in place by a single retainer clip, as a last resort the lock can be punched out. First, insert a bent piece of wire into the keyway and bind it to prevent the lock mechanism from falling into the door frame. Once out, the automobile can be opened by pushing up on the linkage attached to the lock mechanism.

Since vehicle door locks on most of the new models are usually held in place by a retainer clip, a last resort would be to punch the lock out. First insert a bent piece of wire into the keyway, and bind it to prevent the lock mechanism from falling into the door frame. Once out, the vehicle can be opened by pushing up on the linkage attached to the locking mechanism

Plastic packing strap is commonly used to strap retail boxes. Obtain a section about one metre long. Bend it in half, and make it flat, either by biting it, or hitting it with a hammer. Take the plastic strap, and force it past the rubber seal where the door opens, through the door, or around the window. Now you just manipulate the plastic strap to the Button Lock on the inside of the door. Try to hook it, once you have hooked the button lock, simply Pull Up. It works best when going in at the top of the window.

If all else fails, a side window (usually driver's side) can be broken almost silently using either a specialised spring-loaded glass breaker or a small piece of porcelain from a spark plug – this method is preferred as all it takes is for the operator to toss or flick a gravel sized piece of porcelain at the car window as he or she walks by, which will crack the security glass.

All that is needed is to carefully rake the safety glass out of the window frame onto a tarp or coat.

Keyless Ignition and steering lock defeat

As long as the vehicle is not a modern type fitted with a transponder, keyless ignition is relatively simple. There are several methods of keyless ignition and these will be described in detail below.

Hotwiring: It is quite possible to receive an electric shock while hotwiring a vehicle. The risk of shock can be avoided by not touching any bare wires. It should also be noted that many modern types of vehicle are equipped with security devices which prevent hotwiring. The method described below is effective on almost all older models.

1.   **Put the car in the proper gear.** If it's a manual - put it in neutral and make sure the parking break is on. If it's an automatic, make sure it's in park.

2.   **Open the bonnet/hood and find the coil wire.** To find it follow the plug wires. For V8 engines, these wires are usually located at the rear of engine. For V6, they are usually on the left-center. For Four-cylinder engines, they are usually on the right-center of the engine. Run a wire from the positive side of the battery to the positive side of the coil wire. This should give power to the dash.

3.   **Find the starter solenoid.** At the solenoid you will see a small wire and the positive battery cable. Cross these wires with a set of pliers. The engine should crank.

There are two basic types of cars in use today. The first is the older type (pre 1976) That have the ignition switch built into the dash board. These cars can be hotwired in a number of ways depending on the knowledge and skill level of the operator.

The fastest way is to run a wire from the positive pole on the battery to the positive side to the coil. The battery and the coil will be marked with a + sign. After connecting the wire, you will need to jump the starter. On some vehicles, This is done from under the car. There will be one thick wire and two thin wires. Just use a screw driver and connect the big bolt holding the thick wire to the thin wire close to the motor. Once these two touch, The starter will turn over and start the car.

On other types of cars (and trucks) there will be a Starter relay on the fender very close to the battery. Just follow the Positive cable till to a round cylinder connected to it. Use the bare metal handles on a pair of pliers to connect the battery wire to the Small wire on the relay. Again, Once these connect, The motor will turn over. Be sure to hook the wire to the battery first. Any sparks near the battery may cause the fumes coming from the battery to ignite.

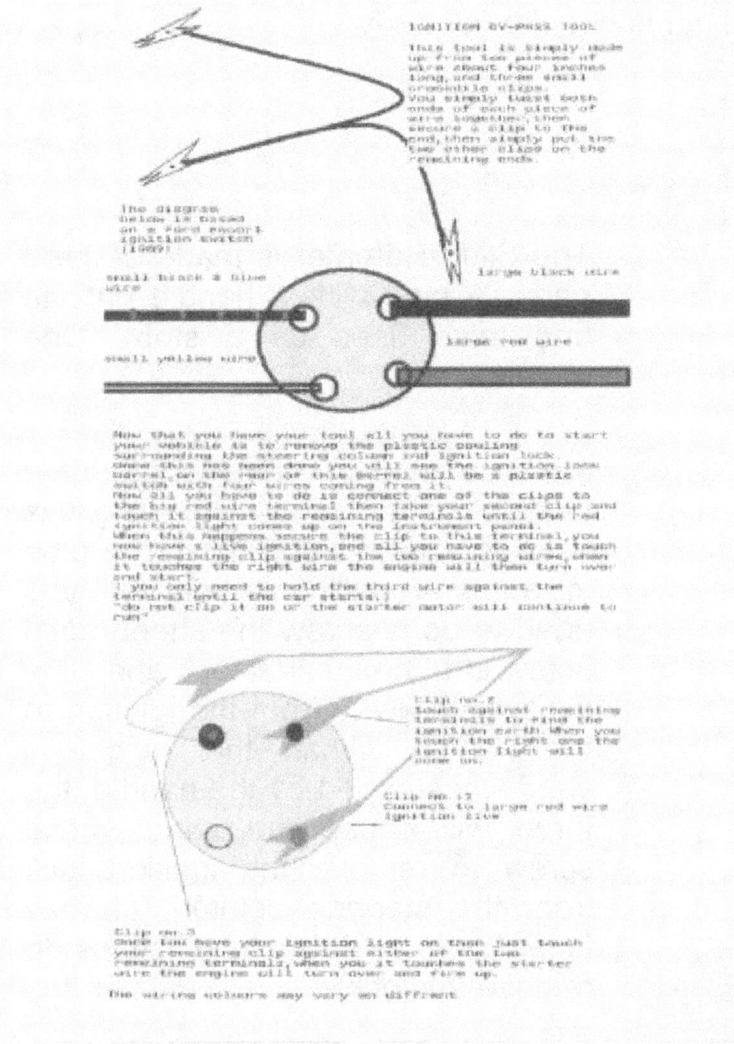

The under the dash board hot wire is in

some ways more difficult to execute, but it is preferable to the possible compromise risk which may occur from the operator attempting to hotwire

from under the

bonnet/hood. There are 5 wires going into the ignition. The only one that remains the same colour on all cars is the red one. This is the main hot wire for the whole ignition. The fastest way to know what is what is to remember that all the wires but one can be connected

at one time. The first thing to do is find is the starter wire.

Cut and strip all the wires. Then one at a time touch them to the red wire. When the starter turns over you have identified the correct wire. Connect all the other wires to the red one. This will activate the ignition and all accessories. Then all that is needed is to touch the starter wire to the bundle of wires just long enough to start the car. To stop the engine, disconnect the wires.

The newer types of vehicles have the ignition switch built into the steering column. This was done as an anti-theft deterrent. With the ignition switch built into the steering column, The easiest and fastest way to start one of these vehicles is to obtain (or build) what is known as a Slide Hammer. This is used in auto panel beaters/body shops and can be bought in a parts store for about $15.00-$75.00. It is designed to pull dents out of a car body.

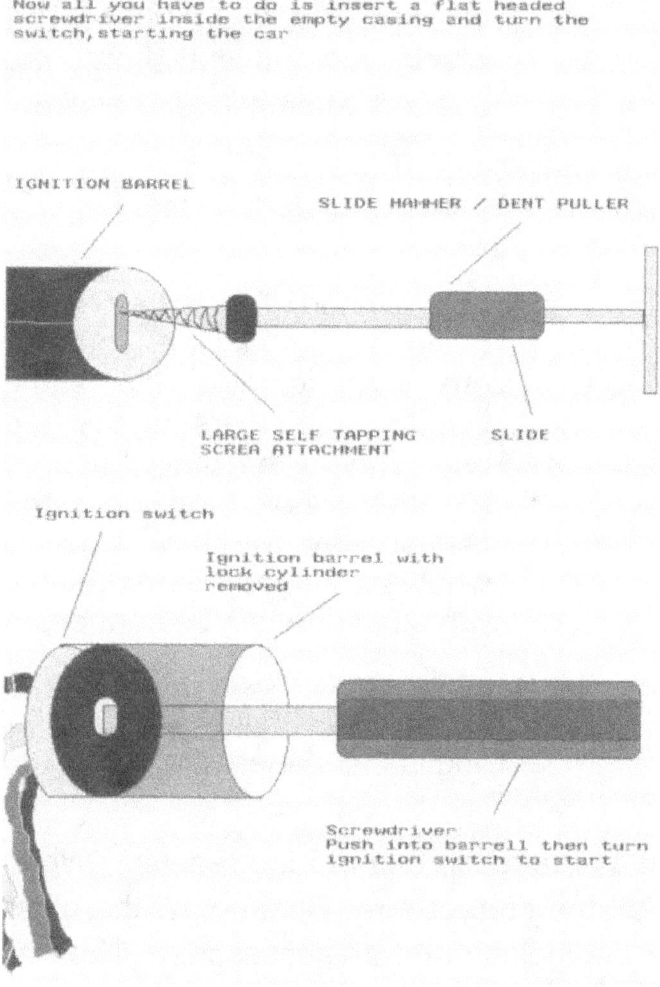

The Slide Hammer is made of three parts. A pipe with a handle on one and (also used as a stop). One sheet metal screw (Normally welded to the pipe). And a weight. The weight is used to slide up and down the pipe to apply a pulling action. All you need to do is screw the sheet metal screw into the ignition lock and slide the weight away from the ignition to the handle. When the weight is suddenly stopped by the handle, the force will cause the sheet metal screw to remove the ignition lock from the steering column. (it may take 2 or 3 good hard blows to remove the lock).

Once the lock is removed, Insert a regular screw driver into the aperture

where the lock was originally installed. You will see a slot (almost like a screw). Once the screw driver is in, Just turn the screw driver clockwise and the starter will turn. If you wish to stop the motor, Just do the same but turn the screw driver counter clockwise.

A variation of this method is to simply hammer a suitably-sized flat-nosed screwdriver into the ignition keyway, breaking the lock pins and disengaging the steering lock. Turn the screwdriver clockwise to crank the ignition.

Vehicle Alarm & Immobilizer Issues

Although alarmed vehicles are to be avoided due to the extra time it takes to defeat some of the more sophisticated systems, some situations may arise where an alarmed vehicle is the only option for the team to extract the immediate area.

With the variety of different aftermarket vehicle accessories released by different manufacturers available worldwide, alarm systems encountered in the field will differ. This section will describe generic methods which may work. Experimentation is the key.

The simplest technique is to remove the front indicator lens of the target vehicle and smash the bulb. A screwdriver or insulated knife blade is then used to short the bulb contacts. If this is done correctly, there is a chance that the fuse will blow. As most generic brands of car alarm have the alarm on the same circuit as the indicators, the alarm may either cease or not activate at all.

Most alarm systems are wired to a door pressure release switch. The wiring for this alarm trip is usually located within the bundle of wires which contains the central locking, power window and interior light cabling. Using a wooden or plastic wedge, it is possible to slightly wedge open the gap between the front door and the side pillar in most vehicles. If a ongl serrated blade such as a standard kitchen knife were slid into this gap, the cabling could be cut and the alarm short circuited with the knife blade. Once the door is opened using standard door entry techniques (wire hanger, packing strap, removal of door locks, etc.), the vehicle can be hotwired or otherwise started.

Be aware that the above methods may not be effective on modern types of vehicles and they may not disarm a vehicle immobilizer. Unfortunately, there are few reliable ways of circumventing an immobilizer and these ways are specific to certain types. The team would be better served to seek alternate transport when faced with an apparent immobilizer threat.

Tools

Slide Hammer:

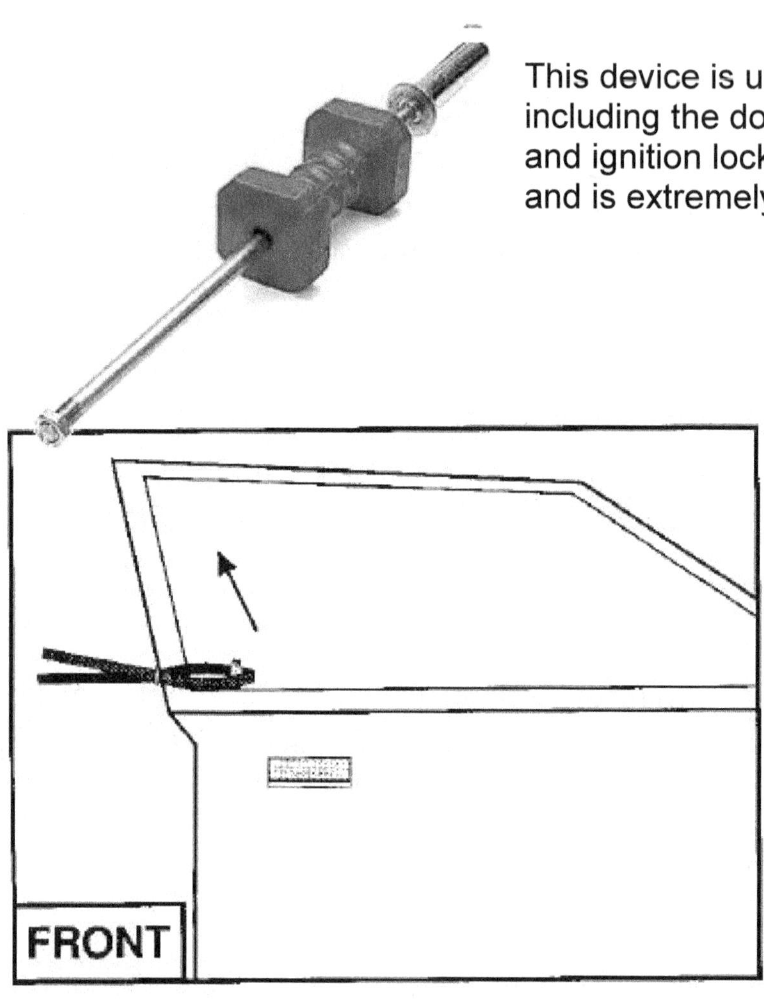

This device is used to remove vehicle locks, including the door locks, boot/trunk lock, and ignition lock. The tool is simple to use and is extremely effective.

Packing Strap: This tool is easily obtained and is used to lift the door lock knob on older style vehicles. Very effective.

1. Insert the No. 100 into vehicle between door and weatherstripping.
2. Slide one end of tool forward to form loop over lock button.
3. Pull tool tight around lock button.
4. Lift tool up to unlock door.

NOTE: No. 100 is a basic piece of packing tape

Driving and Security Precautions

While in transit, the team should drive at the same pace and in the same manner as the surrounding vehicles. In some countries, it is abnormal for a vehicle to travel the speed limit and police in these areas may see a car which is not speeding as one which is trying to avoid police attention.

The team should have a plan to deal with police attention. This can include securing good quality fake or stolen drivers permits, or even interdiction of police as they approach the vehicle. All possible eventualities and escape routes should be discussed and planned prior to the operation.

When parked or propped, the vehicle should be in a position which is not suspicious. A lone vehicle on an empty street in the early hours of the morning is bound to attract the attention of the target or the local police. If possible use a car park or other crowded place.

Commandeering by use of force

Commonly known in legal circles as "Carjacking" commandeering by use of force means stealing a vehicle while it is being operated by a driver. This is an emergency technique used when alternate transport is not available. The use of this technique entails extra planning such as securing the original driver and strategies to ensure that the theft is not quickly reported to local authorities before the team is able to obtain other transport. It is to be used as a short-term transport solution only.

As a general rule, it is not effective for a team member to simply stand in the middle of the road pointing a weapon at an oncoming vehicle. This may cause the driver to panic and swerve either at the operator or off the road, crashing the vehicle. There are several techniques which can be used:

In an extreme emergency, the team can gain entry to a private premise with a vehicle in the driveway and force the homeowner to supply the keys. The disadvantage of this method is that the theft will usually be reported almost immediately unless the home owner is secured or taken along with the team.

In areas with underground carparks, residential gates, etc. The team may ambush a driver as they stop for the gates. In most cases, threats of violence by team members will only delay entry to the vehicle. The most efficient way to enter a stationary vehicle is to smash the driver's side window and either open the door or drag the drver out through the broken window. As with the above, this type of vehicle commandeering is sure to be reported soon after the fact.

A similar technique can be used when the target vehicle is stopped at traffic lights.

Vehicles can be commandeered at petrol stations, truckstops, car washes and ATM machines.

Trade or delivery vehicles can be commandeered when they are delivering goods (sometimes lured to a specific location).

Vehicle Disposal

There are many ways to dispose of a vehicle once it has served its usefulness. The method of disposal will be determined by the risk to the team presented by the successful recovery of the vehicle by local authorities, which will in turn be determined by the precise mission tasked to the team.

If fingerprints, DNA, etc. are not an issue for whatever reason, often the quickest way to dispose of a vehicle is to dump it in a "hard" area of the host city with the keys in the ignition. This vehicle will probably end up stolen rather quickly and may be reduced to parts or rebirthed by the thieves for profit.

If trace evidence such as fibres, fingerprints and DNA are an issue, the team has one option for vehicle disposal, which is to incinerate the car. This can be most easily accomplished by fuel incendiary placed under one of the front seats of the vehicle initiated with a simple timer. Upon ignition, the fuel will destroy the interior of the vehicle, thus removing any useable forensic evidence.

DNA may also be destroyed by using household bleach. As a useful aside, household bleach will also provide a "false-positive" when the interior of a vehicle is under forensic examination for blood/fluids by the use of the Luminol agent. The interior of a bleach-soaked vehicle will appear to be totally soaked with blood, but the forensic examiner will be unable to localize the blood stain itself, which is useful for assassination operations.

APPENDIX A :

NIGHT VISION GOGGLE DRIVING OPERATIONS

Night Vision Goggles - General Characteristics

NVGs are devices that make an object more visible during periods of low light levels. Performance is directly related to the amount of available light, such as starlight and moonlight. NVGs are passive devices which means that they give off little visual signature which can be detected. In fact, the only way for an adversary to detect an operator who is wearing NVGs is if they look directly into

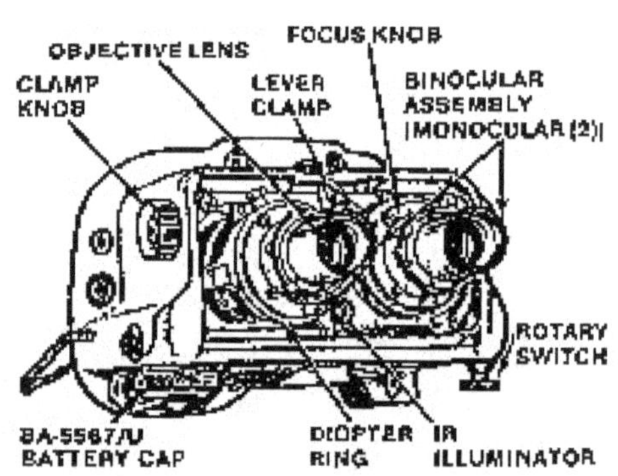

the tubes with another night vision device. The adversary will see two bright points of light similar to an animal's eyes at night. This phenomenon is known as retro-reflectivity.

Sources of Ambient Light
o   The Moon o   Background Lighting o   Artificial Lights o   Solar Lights

NVG use gives a better view of the surrounding area and object identification during low light levels. NVGs make it possible to read, patrol, provide medical aid, drive, walk, and observe the enemy at night without the help of lights.

NVG performance is reduced in rain, haze, fog, snow, or smoke. Also, NVGs do not magnify images viewed through the tubes. An object viewed through the goggles at night will be the same size as if it were seen during the day without the goggles. Objects that are difficult to see during the day with the naked eye are also hard to detect at night with NVGs.

Due to the narrow field of vision, NVGs adversely affect depth perception and the field of view. A driver with 20/20 vision using NVGs will have, at best, 20/50 vision with the NVGs. The field of view with the NVGs is 40 degrees compared to 200 degrees unaided. NVGs provide their best depth perception between 20 to 500 feet. NVGs decrease depth perception at distances less than 20 feet or greater than 500 feet. Depth perception capability for NVGs will be less than daytime unaided but better than nighttime unaided.

__WARNING:__ After wearing the device for a short period, the user begins to feel he has complete visual acuity and depth perception when in fact he does not.

Operate the goggle under nighttime conditions only. To prevent damage to the tubes, operate the NVG in high light conditions only if day vision filters or objective lens caps are attached.

All objects viewed through the NVGs will appear as a single color, green or yellow, depending upon the NVGs' construction. NVGs do not provide for color discrimination. As a result, it is difficult to distinguish between certain objects or features. Shadows, for example, are difficult to distinguish from puddles of water, walls, ditches, and vice versa when viewed through the goggles at night. **It is critical that drivers take the lack of color discrimination into account when using NVGs.**

Upon reentering a high ambient light environment after wearing the NVG for an extended time, you may experience a tint or discoloration of objects viewed with the unaided eye. This is a normal physical reaction that causes no discomfort and disappears after a short time.

Second versus third generation tubes.

There are two distinct generations (models) of NVG tubes with militarily significant performance differences: second and third.

(1) All AN/PVS-5 NVG tubes are second generation. AN/PVS-7 tubes were produced in both second and third generation versions.

(2) Third generation tubes have increased performance and longer tube life (about 7,500 hours). When they eventually fail, they tend to fail quickly.

(3) Second generation tubes have a tube life projected at about 2,500 hours.
They tend to fail slowly, so it is important that maintenance personnel check the devices periodically.

NVG Driving Techniques And Procedures

Effects of light.

NVG compatibility is best achieved by eliminating all interior and exterior vehicle lighting.

WARNING: *Vehicle drivers without NVGs may not see you.*

Instruments and gauges can be read with NVGs without the aid of instrument lighting. Viewing an area lit by artificial lights, such as security floodlights, will limit your ability to see objects outside the lighted area. Try to keep the light source outside the field of view of the goggles. Using goggles will allow you to detect light sources at great distances that are not visible to the unaided eye; for example, flashlights, burning cigarettes, chemical lightsticks, and IR light sources. The capability of goggles to detect these light sources improves as the ambient light level decreases.

Weather considerations when driving with NVGs.

The effectiveness of NVGs is greatly reduced in rain, haze, fog, snow, and/or smoke. NVGs also have a limited ability to detect rain, haze, or fog before you enter the area of reduced visibility.

Visual clues to the presence of visibility restrictions include— *A halo around artificial lights as seen through the goggles.*

An? increase in "image noise" (similar in appearance to the "snow" seen on television with poor reception).

Ground speed limitations.

The normal tendency of most drivers is to overdrive their capability to see! To avoid obstacles, you must understand the relationship between the NVG visual range capability and speed of your vehicle.

Other factors that you must consider to drive at a safe speed when wearing NVGs are:

- Type of NVG being used for driving, and the generation of the image intensifier tube (second or third).

- Type of vehicle used for training.

- Weather conditions.

- Mode of driving, such as convoy and off-road.

- Terrain.

- Amount of light available (natural and artificial).

Vehicle preparation.

Keep windshields clean. Remove dirt, grease, and bugs. Turn off all exterior and interior lights. Tape over those, which cannot be turned off.

Driving with goggles.

The ability to drive with goggles is developed through continuous hands-on training. The key to that training lies in awareness and understanding of NVG capabilities and limitations.

WARNING: NVGs should never be used on public highways. The effect of oncoming headlights on the device may cause some very dangerous situations as the operator will not be able to see other objects in the field of view. If the light is sufficiently bright, the devices all have a bright source protection feature that shuts down the NVG to protect it. If the bright source protection is activated, the NVG will be off for at least 2 seconds. In addition, drivers without NVGs are unlikely to see your vehicle.

Sometimes the above conditions are unavoidable. To minimize the effect on NVGs by the headlights from an oncoming vehicle while avoiding a potentially serious accident, do the following:

1. Slow down,

2. Look away so that the light source is just outside the goggles field of view, and

3. Pull off to the far left-hand side of the road (use caution when pulling to the side of the road to avoid an unintended departure from the roadway).

4. NVG use at this point is now compromised as other vehicles with headlights on may appear. Do not continue driving with NVGs.

In the event of a malfunction, follow these procedures:

1.   If your vehicle malfunctions or if the NVGs exhibit faults such as shading, flashing, or flickering, slow down and pull off to the side of the road.

2.   If the NVGs low battery indicator turns on, replace the batteries. Do not wait until the goggles shut down while driving because of weak or dead batteries. Slow down and pull off to the side of the road

Since the field of view is greatly reduced, you must use a slow, continual scanning pattern to compensate for this.

Operating a vehicle with the goggles over a tactical respirator (gas mask) will further reduce your field of vision to about 20 degrees. (This practice is not recommended.)

All NVG driving operations should be conducted with the NVG secured in the head harness and worn on the driver's head.

Motorcycles and ATVs may be operated with NVGs. In general, the motorcycle or ATV should be operated with headlights off. The additional weight that the goggles place on the operator's head and the position of this weight may require ATV and motorcycle operators to redevelop their sense of balance during training.

The limited field of view of NVGs will have a greater impact on motorcycle and ATV operators than on other vehicles. Operators will have to practice and train to turn their heads from side to side to compensate for the loss of peripheral vision.

TACTICAL VEHICLE OPERATION COURSE SCHEDULES

1-Day Special Operations Evasive Driving Course

0900-1000 **Barricade Breaching and** **Drivable Terrain**	Ramming through a car that is blocking your path both forward and in reverse. Driving off the road as a means of escape.
1000-1100 **Evasive Manoeuvres**	Forward and reverse 180-degree turns including limited space and curved road scenarios.
1100-1200 **Vehicle Intervention Practical**	The Precision Immobilization Technique (PIT) is the most efficient and safest way to stop a fleeing vehicle. Students are shown this manoeuvre so they know how to defend against it.

1200-1300 **Lunch**	
1300-1330 **Attack Recognition Lecture**	The importance of being mentally prepared in order to execute an escape manoeuvre.
1330-1400 **Forward and Reverse 180-Degree Turn Practice**	
1400-1500 **Barricade Confrontations Practical**	Students come under simulated attack and must choose and execute the correct escape manoeuvre.
1500-1700 **Defensive Line**	Protection from being stopped while fleeing from an attacker. Students come under attack through actual contact exercises and are required to use their automobile as a weapon to protect themselves.

1-Day Special Operations Advanced Driving Course

0900-0930 **Vehicle Dynamics Lecture**	Understanding the driver/vehicle relationship. Vehicle language, driving form, weight transfer, ocular driving, threshold braking and off-road recoveries.
0930-1030 **Vehicle Dynamics Practical I**	Students practice these skills through serpentine and emergency braking exercises. Surprise off-road recoveries are conducted throughout the day.
1030-1100 **Vehicle Dynamics Lecture II**	Skid control and spin recovery. Understanding oversteer and understeer, and how they are controlled. How tire pressure affects performance and how to prevent blowouts.

1100-1200 **Vehicle Dynamics Practical II**	Skid control (oversteer and understeer) and advanced emergency threshold braking.
1200-1300 **Lunch**	
1300-1330 **Vehicle Dynamics Lecture III**	Understanding multiple dynamics, braking, braking in curves, and swerving-to-avoid obstacles.
1330-1430 **Vehicle Dynamics Practical III**	Emergency braking in turns and swerve-to-avoid obstacles.

1430-1500 **Technical Drive and Mental Aspects Lecture**	The laws of vehicle dynamics are applied to allow vehicle control at above highway speeds. Techniques of stress management are discussed.
1500-1600 **Technical Drive Practical**	The laws of vehicle dynamics are applied to maintain control at emergency speeds.
1600-1700 **Technical Drive Final**	Students are asked to drive at emergency speeds under pressure, applying acquired skills.
After Sunset **Night Drive Lecture**	The limitations of vision and lighting. Driving with Night Observation Devices.

One Hour **Night Drive Practical**	Technical driving skills are applied along with visual limitations.

www.ingramcontent.com/pod-product-compliance
Lightning Source LLC
Chambersburg PA
CBHW080856260726
48660CB00009B/3318